THE FOUR OF US

"Not only funny and moving, it's surprising."
—TOBY ZINMAN, *The Philadelphia Inquirer*

"[Moses] cements his status as the most self-consciously clever among the current crop of young playwrights." —BOB VERINI, *Variety*

"The swaggering pulse of this play is the torrent of imagination and perception just beginning to hit full flow from an author with a hearty potential for a long and productive career."
—WELTON JONES, sandiego.com

BACH AT LEIPZIG

"[An] intellectual fun house of a play [that becomes] a poignant meditation on the artistic temperament and the transporting power of music." —CELIA WREN, *The Washington Post*

"Brashly sophisticated, cuttingly comic, boldly brainy, verbally baroque, structurally complex and altogether virtuosic."
—HEDY WEISS, *Chicago Sun-Times*

"[A] funny, fiercely intelligent romp."
—F. KATHLEEN FOLEY, *Los Angeles Times*

"Moses clearly has a playful mind, an adventurous breadth of curiosity and a delightful appreciation of the tension between form and meaning." —LINDA WINER, *Newsday*

Itamar Moses | THE FOUR OF US

ITAMAR MOSES is the author of the full-length plays *Outrage, Bach at Leipzig* (Faber, 2005), *Celebrity Row, Yellowjackets, Back Back Back*, and *Completeness*, and various short plays and one-acts. His work has appeared Off-Broadway and elsewhere in New York, at regional theaters across the country, and in Canada. He has received new play commissions from the McCarter Theatre, Playwrights Horizons, Berkeley Repertory Theatre, Wilma Theater, Manhattan Theatre Club, and South Coast Repertory. Moses holds an MFA in Dramatic Writing from New York University and has taught playwriting there and at Yale. He is a member of the Dramatists Guild, MCC Playwrights' Coalition, and Naked Angels Mag-7, and is a New York Theatre Workshop Usual Suspect. Born in Berkeley, California, Moses now lives in Brooklyn.

ALSO BY ITAMAR MOSES

Bach at Leipzig

The FOUR of US

The FOUR of US

A PLAY

Itamar Moses

WITHDRAWN

FABER AND FABER, INC.
An affiliate of Farrar, Straus and Giroux
New York

FABER AND FABER, INC.

An affiliate of Farrar, Straus and Giroux

18 West 18th Street, New York 10011

Library of Congress Cataloging-in-Publication Data

Moses, Itamar, 1977–

The four of us / Itamar Moses. — 1st ed.

   p. cm.

ISBN-13: 978-0-86547-989-0 (pbk. : alk. paper)

ISBN-10: 0-86547-989-5 (pbk. : alk. paper)

   1. Authors—Drama.   2. Male friendship—Drama.   3. Success—Drama.

I. Title.

PS3613.077889F68 2008

812'.6—dc22

2007045428

Designed by Cassandra J. Pappas

www.fsgbooks.com

1   3   5   7   9   10   8   6   4   2

Because I was having withdrawals.

Remember?

Acknowledgments

No list like this can ever be complete, but here is my attempt at a partial one. Joanna Pfaelzer, Carey Perloff, and the folks at A.C.T. in San Francisco gave this play its initial workshop, in which Cody Nickell and Johnathan McClain brought these characters vividly to life for the very first time and helped me to find and shape them. Jerry Patch and the Old Globe Theatre in San Diego gave the play its first full production, with Sean Dugan and Gideon Banner, who did beautiful work that deepened with every performance while rolling with all the changes, large and small, that I continued to make up through previews. Both these incarnations were directed by Pam Mackinnon, with whom I by now have a rehearsal room rapport that borders on telepathy, which is no small thing. Other aid along the way came from Mandy Hackett, Michelle Tattenbaum, Daniel Goldstein, and Stephen Willems. The efforts of my agent, Mark Christian Subias, on behalf of this play have been predictably tireless. Lynne Meadow, Paige Evans, Dan Sullivan, and everyone at Manhattan Theatre Club have made me feel like a member of their family as we prepare for the play's New York opening. Thanks also to Denise Oswald and everyone at Faber and Faber for making it possible for my plays to live also as books.

The FOUR of US

PRODUCTION HISTORY

The Four of Us had its world premiere at the Old Globe Theatre in San Diego on February 8, 2007. Director: Pam MacKinnon. Set Designer: Kris Stone. Lighting Designer: Russell Champa. Sound Designer: Paul Peterson. Costume Designer: Marcus Henry. Director of Production: Robert Drake. Stage Manager: Tracy Skoczelas.

DAVID   Sean Dugan
BENJAMIN   Gideon Banner

The Four of Us was originally produced in New York by the Manhattan Theatre Club on March 6, 2008. Lynne Meadow, Artistic Director; Barry Grove, Executive Producer; Daniel Sullivan, Acting Artistic Director for the 2007–2008 Season. Director: Pam MacKinnon. Assistant Director: Dominic D'Andrea. Scenic and Costume Design: David Zinn. Lighting Design: Russell H. Champa. Sound Design: Daniel Baker. Production Manager: Kurt Gardner. Production Stage Manager: Robyn Henry. Stage Manager: Nicole Bouclier.

DAVID   Michael Esper
BENJAMIN   Gideon Banner

CHARACTERS

DAVID, friends with Benjamin.
BENJAMIN, friends with David.

They appear between the ages of seventeen and twenty-seven, though not in that order.

SCENE ONE

(An Indian restaurant.)

*(*DAVID *and* BENJAMIN, *both twenty-four, have just finished lunch. The bill is on the table.)*

BENJAMIN: What do you mean?

DAVID: I, uh, *have* something for you. Here, let me . . .

*(*DAVID *begins to rummage in his bag.)*

BENJAMIN: What, like a present?

DAVID: Kind of.

BENJAMIN: Oh, oh, that's—

DAVID: In, uh, in honor of the occasion.

BENJAMIN: You're already taking me to *lunch*, you don't have
to—

DAVID: No, no, don't worry. It was simple. And *free*. I'm resourceful like that.

(DAVID *stands a photograph in a simple wooden frame on the table.*)

BENJAMIN: What's this? *(Pause.)* Is that me?

DAVID: Yeah, that's you, uh . . . at work. On the book.

BENJAMIN: Right.

DAVID: So that's you . . . finishing it, I guess.

BENJAMIN: I didn't finish it until I got back to school. Remember, you came to visit.

DAVID: So: starting it. I forget which. Anyway, it seemed appropriate.

BENJAMIN: Where did you *find* this?

DAVID: What do you mean? I took it out of my photo album from, from Prague, from that summer.

BENJAMIN: Ah.

DAVID: That's the problem with spending a summer in a country where you don't know anybody? With just one friend? All my pictures are of you.

BENJAMIN: Well, we can probably assume that all mine are of you.

DAVID: We probably can.

(Beat.)

BENJAMIN: Though, actually, I never got mine together into an album.

DAVID: No?

BENJAMIN: No, they're all in some shoe box in my parents' house. *(Beat.)* What did you write that summer?

DAVID: I, uh . . . What do you . . . ? A *play*.

BENJAMIN: No, I figured, but: which one?

DAVID: The one about the, uh . . . You know what? It was terrible.

BENJAMIN: I'm sure it wasn't.

DAVID: It was. I was an undergraduate. I had just read Ruskin for the first time and I for some reason thought that his ideas about Gothic architecture in *The Stones of Venice* might make a good subject for a play. It was terrible.

BENJAMIN: You don't know that it was terrible.

DAVID: I saw it. I put it up at school that fall.

BENJAMIN: Maybe it was ruined by the director.

DAVID: I directed it myself. Because nobody else would. Because it was terrible. Like, two weeks ago? Becca saw it on my shelf and asked to read it? And I let her read *everything*. And I was like, "No, please. It's *terrible*."

BENJAMIN: Well, maybe it . . . paved the way for something good later on.

DAVID: We can only hope.

(Beat.)

BENJAMIN: How *is* Rebecca?

DAVID: Good. Uh, really good.

BENJAMIN: Things are good?

DAVID: Things are really good. It's . . . getting kind of serious.

BENJAMIN: And you're good with that.

DAVID: I'm *great* with that. No feelings of emotional claustrophobia, no inexplicable depression, no anxiety attacks, it's a whole new . . . phase for me. Someone to share my popcorn at the movies.

BENJAMIN: You're very fortunate.

DAVID: Thanks. I know. Thank you. We should all get together.

BENJAMIN: Who?

DAVID: You, me, Bec, and Emily. For dinner, or something.

BENJAMIN: Oh. Uh . . .

DAVID: What.

BENJAMIN: We kind of broke up, actually.

DAVID: What?

BENJAMIN: Me and Emily.

DAVID: Are you *serious?*

BENJAMIN: Yeah.

DAVID: *When?*

BENJAMIN: I guess . . . a little over a month ago.

DAVID: *What?*

BENJAMIN: Yeah.

DAVID: *Really.*

BENJAMIN: Uh. Yeah.

DAVID: Ben!

BENJAMIN: What?

DAVID: Just . . . *Oh. (Pause.)* Uh. Why?

BENJAMIN: Um. What do you mean?

DAVID: For what reason?

BENJAMIN: It was . . . time. It was just time.

DAVID: How long had you guys been together?

BENJAMIN: Four years. Four years on and off.

DAVID: And it was just . . . *time.*

BENJAMIN: There were . . . Let's say it became clear that there were things that maybe each of us wasn't going to be able to offer the other? That we maybe needed? Which had been fine in the past and was in fact still fine in the present but would pretty clearly *not* be fine at some point in the future? And so it was just . . . time. *(Pause.)* So.

DAVID: Do you want to talk about it?

BENJAMIN: What do you mean?

DAVID: I . . . don't actually know. Are you okay?

BENJAMIN: I think so. Yeah, I'm fine. *(Pause.)* I mean, I had a little bit of a hard time. When it first . . . Actually, I tried to call you. *(Pause.)* I left you a whole series of messages, actually.

DAVID: Right, yeah. I was, you know . . . I was out of town.

BENJAMIN: I know. It's fine. But, so, by now, I'm sort of . . .

(BENJAMIN shrugs. He is fine.)

DAVID: Okay. Well, so, but if you . . .

BENJAMIN: What?

DAVID: I don't know. I guess . . . Okay.

BENJAMIN: Thanks, though. *(Beat. The photo:)* I mean, *thank* you. This is . . . very nice.

DAVID: You're welcome.

BENJAMIN: I should probably put it away now, though.

DAVID: No, you should totally just leave it. And just be staring at this picture of yourself when the waiter comes over to get the money—

BENJAMIN: Right: "He brings it to every meal. It helps him to digest."

(BENJAMIN puts the photo away. DAVID picks up the bill and looks it over.)

BENJAMIN: You really don't have to do that.

DAVID: I said I would. That was the deal.

BENJAMIN: I . . . guess it was. *(Pause.)* So where were you?

DAVID: What?

BENJAMIN: When you were out of town.

DAVID: Oh. I . . . Didn't I tell you? I was a counselor.

BENJAMIN: Where?

DAVID: A, uh, a camp counselor. At . . . This is funny . . . At Young Musicians.

BENJAMIN: No kidding. What was that like?

DAVID: It was . . . trippy. I mean, the place hasn't changed at all, and the kids are exactly the same, I mean, kid for kid, you can sort of match people up, there's the younger version of each person *we* were there with, you know. You remember.

BENJAMIN: Vividly.

DAVID: Right. *(Old-man wistful)* "The summer we met."

BENJAMIN: It was.

DAVID: And it was especially . . . I mean, I don't know about you, but I was always kind of wondering what the counselors were thinking? Of the kids. Like, what they thought of *us*, if they thought any of us were going to be great superfamous rock star musicians, like we all thought we were gonna be? And it was weird. To *know*. That, in fact, the counselors are thinking: Wow, some of these girls are pretty cute.

BENJAMIN: Right.

DAVID: And also they were thinking: Ninety-nine percent of you will give up music entirely sometime in the next ten years.

BENJAMIN: Like we did.

DAVID: Like we did.

BENJAMIN: So . . . why did you work there?

DAVID: For fun. And, you know: grad school. Free summers. I needed the money. And: grad school for *playwriting*, you don't work as an investment banker.

BENJAMIN: Right.

(Pause.)

DAVID: So . . . what happens now?

BENJAMIN: What do you mean?

DAVID: To . . . I don't know. It's supposed to be this watershed thing, but what actually *happens*. To someone like *you*.

BENJAMIN: What do you mean to someone like me?

DAVID: I just mean: to someone specific who I know personally, I guess, as opposed to the abstract idea of a hypothetical first-time author who has sold a hypothetical first novel.

BENJAMIN: Well, I think in this case it will be the whole . . . apparatus.

DAVID: The whole . . . ?

BENJAMIN: Just . . . reviews. Public readings. A lot of those, probably.

DAVID: Okay.

BENJAMIN: Just because the publisher is sort of in a position where extensive promotion is probably smart.

DAVID: Oh.

BENJAMIN: And, you know, a book tour.

DAVID: Like an actual *tour*.

BENJAMIN: What do you mean?

DAVID: Of places all across the country.

BENJAMIN: Of, well, of several countries.

DAVID: Of *several* countries.

BENJAMIN: Well, of the countries in which the book is being published.

DAVID: How many is *that*?

BENJAMIN: I don't . . . You know, I don't know the exact number offhand.

DAVID: So . . . More than two?

BENJAMIN: Well . . .

DAVID: So you're leaving *town*?

BENJAMIN: Not for a while. I mean, you know, the wheels turn pretty slow. It'll be a year before the thing comes out, and *then* I'll go.

DAVID: How long are you going to be gone?

BENJAMIN: Well, intermittently. But for a year or so. And then the paperback comes out. So: two years.

DAVID: What about your *job*?

BENJAMIN: I quit my job.

DAVID: Oh. *(Pause.)* Okay. Um. *(Pause.)* Look, I've been refraining from asking. Out of . . . I don't know. *Decorum.* But.

BENJAMIN: *(He knows what's coming.)* Um . . .

DAVID: How much money are we talking about exactly?

BENJAMIN: I'd . . . rather not say.

DAVID: You don't have to be embarrassed.

BENJAMIN: Um. I'm not.

DAVID: So tell me.

BENJAMIN: I just, I think . . . No.

DAVID: Okay.

BENJAMIN: Is that okay?

DAVID: That is . . . just fine.

(DAVID *takes a sip of water.*)

BENJAMIN: Two million dollars.

(DAVID *spits a mouthful of water all over* BENJAMIN.)

BENJAMIN: Jesus.

DAVID: Are you fucking serious?

BENJAMIN: What the hell is wrong with you?

DAVID: I'm sorry. Here, let . . . Take my napkin.

BENJAMIN: I've got one, thanks.

DAVID: I'm so sorry.

BENJAMIN: It's okay.

DAVID: God, I spit *all over* you.

BENJAMIN: Well, that's . . . It's actually sort of the reaction I was expecting, only I imagined it as more figurative and less literal.

DAVID: I'm sorry. *(Pause.)* Are you fucking serious?

BENJAMIN: Yes. I figured you'd . . . read it in the paper, probably, soon, anyway.

DAVID: Uh. *Yeah.*

BENJAMIN: So I figured what the hell.

DAVID: How the fuck did that happen?

BENJAMIN: What do you mean?

DAVID: Uh. How on God's green earth did such a thing take place?

BENJAMIN: Well, the details of the business are pretty dull, actually.

DAVID: I promise you they're not.

BENJAMIN: No, really, it's kind of depressing.

DAVID: What is?

BENJAMIN: The way that this works. It's *very* depressing.

DAVID: Um. How is that?

BENJAMIN: I don't . . . *(Pause.)* All right: you remember that agent I first had? Celeste's agent, who she set me up with?

DAVID: Okay, I know she was your teacher? But it's still so weird to me when you call her Celeste.

BENJAMIN: Why?

DAVID: Because she's sort of an august-famous-novelist personage, and I tend to think of her in terms of her full name and so it's weird.

BENJAMIN: Okay.

DAVID: That's all.

BENJAMIN: So, remember when I was working with her agent? How she'd kind of send the book to publishers one at a time, and as each one turned it down, she'd, you know, she'd move on to the next one?

DAVID: Yeah. You were kinda bummed about that, I . . . Actually, I thought *that's* what all your messages were about, you know, when I checked them from out of town? If I'd known it was about Emily—

BENJAMIN: It's fine.

DAVID: No, really, I'm really really sorry I've been so hard to reach lately, it's been . . . like I said, things with Becca have been getting serious, and *I* was really busy, I've been sending scripts out a lot, trying to, you know—

BENJAMIN: It's fine.

DAVID: No, I know, but—

BENJAMIN: Um. It's really. Really. Fine.

(Pause.)

DAVID: Okay.

BENJAMIN: Okay. So. Yeah, right around while Emily and I were breaking up, I switched to a different agent who has this sort of different approach? Where the manuscript is submitted to maybe a dozen publishers simultaneously, and then, on some designated day, there's, basically, a . . . bidding war. And, I guess, the strength of this approach is that there's a psychology at work, where the very fact that other publishers are making offers creates a sense that it's okay to do so. That *you* don't want to be the one who let it go.

DAVID: And then you go with the one who offers the most money.

BENJAMIN: Um. It depends.

DAVID: In this case two million dollars.

BENJAMIN: Oh, no, no, that's everything together, that's with international rights from all the various—

DAVID: Okay. But, so—

BENJAMIN: Plus the film rights—

DAVID: So . . . *(Beat.)* I'm sorry, *film* rights?

BENJAMIN: Anyway, the *point* is, in *my* case, I went with the publisher that I felt most . . . comfortable with, the, the strongest rapport with the editors. The most . . . at home.

DAVID: So somebody offered *more* than that?

BENJAMIN: Well, no, as it *happened*, it also turned out to be the place that offered the most money, yes.

DAVID: What a coincidence.

BENJAMIN: Well, it's not, not really, if you think about it, because it does speak to a level of passion about the work, and also at that level it's really an investment in the future, because they're never ever going to earn back that advance from the sale of this book, and they know that.

DAVID: Uh-huh.

BENJAMIN: I mean, look, it's not as if doing it the other way doesn't have exactly the same problem.

DAVID: What problem? I didn't say anything.

BENJAMIN: I mean, either way, people will always do the safe thing. If everybody's making offers, the *safe* thing is to make an offer. If they know they're the only publisher looking at it, the safe thing is to reject it. So in *neither* case does it really have to do, really, with the, you know, the extant, objective quality of the book itself, it just has to do with . . . *hype.* And that's not because you're engaging with the business in one particular way, or in another particular way. It's just because you're engaging with the business . . . at *all.* Which is depressing.

DAVID: Right. I guess that's . . . true. *(Pause.)* So what were you doing while this was going on?

BENJAMIN: What.

DAVID: The bidding war.

BENJAMIN: Uh. Answering the phone. Taking notes. *(Pause.)* Feeling increasingly uncomfortable. I don't know.

DAVID: So . . . who bought the *film* rights?

BENJAMIN: Some . . . I don't know. This actor. Some actor. His name didn't mean anything to me.

DAVID: What was it?

BENJAMIN: I don't remember. I don't really follow those things very much.

DAVID: Uh, yes, I know you don't.

BENJAMIN: So, but yeah, I'm supposed to meet with him about it sometime in the next few months. Which I'm sort of dreading.

DAVID: Why?

BENJAMIN: Because I don't really have any interest in being *involved.* I mean, it's not a medium I'm . . . It's a fun idea, but my work on this particular story is done, you know? So . . .

DAVID: So . . . *(Pause.)* I mean, is there a *role* in it he wants to play, or . . . ?

BENJAMIN: I think he maybe wants to direct it? But I actually have no idea really.

DAVID: So . . .

BENJAMIN: What.

DAVID: Nothing. Never mind. *(Beat.)* I mean: Congratulations!

BENJAMIN: Thanks.

DAVID: No, seriously, this is *great*. It is just great. *(Pause.)* It's, uh, it's *amazing*. It's incredibly cool.

BENJAMIN: Thank you.

DAVID: It *is* cool. You know what the coolest thing about it is?

BENJAMIN: Uh. What.

DAVID: That . . . Well, I sort of never had any doubt, you know, for either of us, that we could make lives out of this, doing our writing, and teaching writing, and basically just, you know—

BENJAMIN: Cobble it together.

DAVID: Exactly. Right. Cobble it together. But now you're . . .

BENJAMIN: Sure.

DAVID: *Solvent.* You know? Just from writing. Just . . . to write. Like . . . *forever*.

BENJAMIN: Not forever.

DAVID: Right, but for a *long*, long . . . I mean—

BENJAMIN: No, you're right. And, I think, ultimately, that's got to be the rationale.

DAVID: For what?

BENJAMIN: For . . . these kinds of *sums*.

DAVID: What do you mean?

BENJAMIN: Like, for example: I spoke to the woman who's publishing the book in Spain? And she said to me, she said: "Don't drink. Don't smoke. Exercise. Take care of yourself." And I just thought: What a wonderful thing to say to someone.

(Pause.)

DAVID: Well, it's great. It's really really great.

BENJAMIN: Thank you.

DAVID: *I* just hope that, uh . . . that having that much money just kind of dropped in your lap, you know . . . that much *time* . . . doesn't turn out to be in some way, kind of . . .

BENJAMIN: What?

DAVID: Totally spiritually corrupting.

(Pause.)

BENJAMIN: What are you talking about?

DAVID: You know, I think it probably, I think it's probably not the best thing in that regard.

BENJAMIN: For what?

DAVID: For . . . you know, it . . . it just . . . I think it must just *cheapen* it.

BENJAMIN: Cheapen what?

DAVID: Whatever. That's just what I think.

(Pause.)

BENJAMIN: That's not what you think.

DAVID: What do you mean?

BENJAMIN: You have never in the past said anything that would lead me to believe that that is what you think.

DAVID: Well, sometimes we don't *know* what we really think of something before we are faced with the, the stark reality of it.

I'm not saying it's what I think *now*. I'm just . . . wondering. You are free not to wonder. It is probably in your interests not to do so.

BENJAMIN: Are you okay?

DAVID: Why? Yeah. I'm fine.

(DAVID takes out money and puts it on the bill, signals for the waiter. During which:)

BENJAMIN: You really don't have to—

DAVID: *(Overlapping)* Yeah. Yeah, I do. I said I would.

(Pause.)

BENJAMIN: Hey.

DAVID: What?

BENJAMIN: Do something surprising.

DAVID: What do you mean?

(BENJAMIN picks up his glass of water and brings it close to his lips.)

BENJAMIN: Say something really shocking.

DAVID: Oh. I get it. Ha-ha.

BENJAMIN: Ready?

DAVID: You're not going to do it.

BENJAMIN: Not if you don't say something shocking enough. It's up to you. Ready?

(Pause.)

DAVID: Okay, yeah.

BENJAMIN: Good. Make it good.

DAVID: I will.

BENJAMIN: Okay. *(Pause.)* Here we go.

(BENJAMIN takes a sip of water . . . the lights shift . . . DAVID stands, puts on his coat, puts on his shoulder bag . . . the space changes around them . . .)

SCENE TWO

(Six months after Scene One. The kitchen/living room of a large, expensive apartment. High ceilings, good sunlight casting shadows of the very tall windows across the length of the floor. One wall is covered with index cards of various colors, filled with writing.)

(BENJAMIN is seated at a table, drinking from a glass of water. DAVID has just arrived: his coat is still on and he carries a bag. He is looking around at the walls.)

DAVID: I've never been in an apartment where the owner has so many enormous pictures of his own face on the walls.

BENJAMIN: They're movie posters. He just put up posters from movies he was in.

DAVID: Right, but you'd think he would have taken into account the sheer number of giant images of his own face that would be on his walls as a result. *(He points.)* You see that one?

BENJAMIN: Yes.

DAVID: Did you like it?

BENJAMIN: Oh, the *movie*. No, I didn't see it.

DAVID: Oh. I, uh . . . He was really good.

BENJAMIN: I've seen almost none of his work. We'll be talking about the book, and how to adapt it, and he'll be like, "It's like that scene in blah blah blah . . . You see that one?" And I'm like, no. Actually, when I was at his birthday party last weekend—

DAVID: You went to his *birthday party*?

BENJAMIN: Yeah.

DAVID: Was it, like, full of celebrities?

BENJAMIN: This is what I'm saying: I have no idea.

DAVID: What do you mean?

BENJAMIN: I mean, uh, there were all these people here who I kind of recognized but I had no idea who they were.

DAVID: Like who?

BENJAMIN: Um. I don't know.

DAVID: Well, what were their names?

BENJAMIN: I don't know, nothing really stuck.

DAVID: That's very annoying to me.

BENJAMIN: This one guy, older guy, I ended up standing next to him in the corner at one point, I guess he was there with his wife, and he kind of looked out over the party, you know, people chatting each other up, and he said, sort of philosophically: "Oh, I'm so glad I'm not out there anymore, going to three of these things a week. Sleeping with a different model every night. You can't live that way for long."

DAVID: Yes, that sounds horrific.

BENJAMIN: I know, I was like: I'd nevertheless like the opportunity to try to live that way at least for a short while and see how well I manage.

(Beat.)

DAVID: And how's that working out for you?

BENJAMIN: Well, I'm not really one to kiss and tell.

DAVID: Certainly not.

BENJAMIN: So let's just say that it seems to involve an awful lot of blow jobs.

(Pause.)

DAVID: What's with all the weird shit on his shelves?

BENJAMIN: They're mostly souvenirs, I think, from movies and things he did. Most of the things on his shelves are souvenirs.

DAVID: *(He points to a photo.)* Is that who I think it is?

BENJAMIN: Yeah.

DAVID: He *knows* them?

BENJAMIN: Yeah, I guess.

DAVID: I just bought their new album. Like *just* now. I have it in my bag.

BENJAMIN: Oh.

DAVID: Have you heard it yet?

BENJAMIN: Not really interested.

DAVID: What? Why not?

BENJAMIN: I'm not really into them.

DAVID: *What?*

BENJAMIN: I just—

DAVID: You're the person who *told* me about them. You like *forced* me to listen to them for *hours*.

BENJAMIN: Really?

DAVID: Yes, *really*. You thought they were *amazing*.

BENJAMIN: Well, I guess I don't anymore.

DAVID: Why not?

BENJAMIN: I don't like the new stuff.

DAVID: You just said you haven't heard it.

BENJAMIN: Well, then I don't like the old stuff anymore.

(DAVID points to the wall with the index cards.)

DAVID: What's that?

BENJAMIN: That's, I guess, some screenplay he's working on. Kind of: laid out scene by scene? I guess so he can swap the order around easier if he—

DAVID: Right, no, I know, just: he writes?

BENJAMIN: I guess.

DAVID: Huh. *(Pause.)* Where is he?

BENJAMIN: He's in the other room. He got a phone call right after you buzzed.

DAVID: This is an *apartment*, right?

BENJAMIN: Yes.

DAVID: How *big* is this place?

BENJAMIN: I have no idea.

DAVID: When did you get here?

BENJAMIN: About an hour ago. We had some things to talk over before you got here.

DAVID: Who is he on the phone with?

BENJAMIN: I . . . don't know. *(Beat.)* What do you mean?

DAVID: I don't know. I just wondered if it was . . . somebody else . . . famous.

BENJAMIN: It's his girlfriend, I think.

DAVID: Dude. She's totally famous.

BENJAMIN: Okay.

DAVID: This is so unfair.

BENJAMIN: Why?

DAVID: Because! You have access to all of these people, but you're too pop-culturally ignorant to appreciate it!

BENJAMIN: He's breaking up with her.

DAVID: *What?*

BENJAMIN: Yeah.

DAVID: *Now?*

BENJAMIN: Yeah. I . . . think so.

DAVID: While we're here in his apartment?

BENJAMIN: Um. Yes.

DAVID: Isn't that a little . . .

BENJAMIN: What.

DAVID: Cavalier?

BENJAMIN: I have no idea.

DAVID: I thought they were really serious.

BENJAMIN: Why did you think that?

DAVID: Because I *read* about it. In a reliable entertainment magazine.

BENJAMIN: Oh. *(Pause.)* So it looks like we have a minute.

DAVID: Okay. *(Pause.)* So . . .

BENJAMIN: So. What's new?

DAVID: Uh. Well, okay: soon you may actually have to take me out to lunch at a, uh, at a Japanese-Caribbean fusion place. If you can find one.

BENJAMIN: What are you talking about? *(Pause.)* Oh! Hey!

DAVID: Yeah.

BENJAMIN: Good for you! What happened?

DAVID: This, uh . . . small thing, really, small small thing.

BENJAMIN: Tell me.

DAVID: This little regional theater . . . in, like, Indiana . . . has this playwriting prize. That I won. So. You know: they're going to do one of my plays.

BENJAMIN: That's great!

DAVID: I mean, the thing is, like, more than a *year* off, and the prize is like *five hundred* dollars, I mean, literally, that's what it is but so—

BENJAMIN: Hey, hey: you know what this means.

DAVID: What?

BENJAMIN: That you are now already at a point that most people never, ever get to with this. That is great. Which play is this?

DAVID: Actually, it's the one I wrote that, that summer. In Prague.

BENJAMIN: Which one was that?

(Beat.)

DAVID: The, uh, the architecture one. Ruskin.

BENJAMIN: Right.

DAVID: Yeah, I . . . I don't know, I took another look at it, thought, maybe, you know, hey, *I* don't know how to direct, maybe I *did* ruin it. Thought I'd give my younger self another chance.

BENJAMIN: Right. *(Pause.)* Hey! So: next week. I'll take you out next week.

DAVID: Great.

(Pause.)

BENJAMIN: Shit.

DAVID: What.

BENJAMIN: I . . . I can't, I'm—

DAVID: That's, that's right, you're—

BENJAMIN: I'm leaving. The book is coming out and then I'm leaving on the tour.

DAVID: Right, well: you know—

BENJAMIN: Sure.

DAVID: When you get back.

BENJAMIN: When I get back. Definitely.

DAVID: Okay. *(Pause.)* So, uh . . . Do you want to tell me exactly what I'm doing here?

BENJAMIN: What do you think you're doing here?

DAVID: I don't want to make any assumptions.

BENJAMIN: Do you know what a treatment is?

DAVID: I . . . what, you mean like a screenplay treatment?

BENJAMIN: Yes.

DAVID: Uh. Yes. It's, uh, it's a description of everything that happens in a movie written out in sort of straightforward prose.

BENJAMIN: He wants me to write a treatment for my book. Which I don't have the first idea how to do, or, really, any interest in doing.

DAVID: Okay.

BENJAMIN: So, I was thinking, maybe you'd want to do it? And then, if he liked it, maybe he'd want you to write the whole thing, or at least to collaborate on it, which would be fun.

DAVID: Yeah. That would.

BENJAMIN: And, you know, might at least *pay* you more than what-ever else it is you're working on now.

DAVID: I . . . I'm sure it would.

BENJAMIN: So he just wants to get a sense of who you are, and what your approach to adapting the book would be, and so that's really all this is.

DAVID: Okay. *(Pause.)* But, I mean, are you sure you want to . . .

BENJAMIN: What.

DAVID: I mean, I'm really . . . I've written, like, one and a half screenplays in my life. Which were terrible. You could . . . you could have access . . . through this guy, or just yourself, in your position, you could . . .

BENJAMIN: What.

(DAVID gestures to the wall of index cards.)

DAVID: Why doesn't he do it himself?

BENJAMIN: I . . . don't know. What do you mean?

DAVID: I guess just: why me?

BENJAMIN: Um. I don't know. Why . . . *not* you?

(Pause.)

DAVID: Okay. Thanks. *(Pause.)* Is there anything in particular he wants?

BENJAMIN: If you could do it in ten pages or, he said, preferably eight, or six, that would be ideal.

DAVID: It's a three-hundred-page novel.

BENJAMIN: I'm just telling you what he said.

DAVID: Dude, a treatment—

BENJAMIN: I'm just . . . telling you what he said.

DAVID: Well, okay, a treatment should really be as long and detailed as possible. In, in the, you know, the *golden* age of cinema, or whatever, people wrote treatments that were, like, two hundred pages long.

BENJAMIN: I really don't know the first thing about it.

DAVID: Okay, well, it should really be more detailed than that.

BENJAMIN: Why?

DAVID: To be actually *useful* in the writing of the movie.

BENJAMIN: I don't know what to tell you.

DAVID: I . . . Okay. *(Pause.)* But . . .

BENJAMIN: What.

DAVID: What are we actually doing *here today*?

BENJAMIN: Just talking about it, I guess. About how you would adapt it.

DAVID: Like a pitch.

BENJAMIN: I guess so.

DAVID: Well, I'd really have liked some time to prepare. I mean: it's a totally different medium.

BENJAMIN: I think you're making this too complicated.

DAVID: I'm serious.

BENJAMIN: Um. That's what I'm talking about. Relax.

DAVID: No, listen: not that, as I explained, not that I've ever *done* an adaptation, *but*: storytelling doesn't actually *work* the same way in both. That's why it's always terrible when a movie is too faithful to a book.

BENJAMIN: Sure, but—

DAVID: Look, here's what I mean. Do you remember the last night of camp, the last night at Young Musicians, where we all had dinner in the woods?

BENJAMIN: Sure.

DAVID: And everybody built a bonfire, and the two of us went up to the hill above it, and looked down on it, and had a sort of maudlin farewell?

BENJAMIN: Sure.

DAVID: So if I, or if someone, were to write the *story* of that summer, or whatever, that's the obvious last scene, okay, that's a good *scene*, it has lots of interesting *scenic* elements, the woods and the night and the fire and the vantage of being up on a hill . . . And if you're putting it into a novel, it's going to be narrative, heavy on description, of the sensations of being in the place, and the internal thoughts of the people, and derive its power from the interaction of those things that are available to you as, as the tools of novel writing, with which, you know, I can't explain them so well because it's not what I do. And if it's in a play, it's going to be dialogic, it's going to be talkier, what's happening is going to be happening underneath dialogue, and maybe the sensate elements will come into play, the visual things and stuff, but in a pretty general mood-setting way, and if it's a *movie*, there *won't* be a lot of talking, probably, and the visual elements will totally take over, it's visual storytelling, it'll all be about cutting from the fire, to someone's face, right as they start to say, you know, the *one line* of dialogue that's in the scene, and then panning up to the stars, or whatever, and in all three cases it's the *same scene* at the end of the *same story.* Only everything about it is different.

BENJAMIN: You probably shouldn't say any of that.

DAVID: Why not?

BENJAMIN: You don't want to give him the impression that your plan is to change everything. He likes the book. That's why he bought the rights.

DAVID: What I'm *saying* is that, sort of counterintuitively, a really good, faithful adaptation is one that actually changes the source material a lot.

BENJAMIN: I think you're just going to confuse him.

DAVID: I'm not saying this to *him.* I'm saying this to *you.*

BENJAMIN: Um. Why?

DAVID: Because . . . you're the one in the room with me. *(Pause.)* So I should just tell him that I'm going to slavishly adhere to every last detail?

BENJAMIN: Oh, well, don't do that, there are certain things he *hates*, so—

DAVID: Like what?

BENJAMIN: The point is—

DAVID: Wait, no, don't you think it might be useful for me to know specifically what it is he *hates*?

BENJAMIN: Well, the ending, for example. He thinks the ending is a failure, too crowded, too much going on at once.

DAVID: Okay.

BENJAMIN: His actual words were: "Too much of a cluster fuck."

DAVID: Which is something he knows a lot about. What with all the models.

BENJAMIN: Oh, he's told me stories.

DAVID: Maybe you can act them out for me with a giant stuffed bear.

(Beat.)

BENJAMIN: Look, I feel like you're getting upset.

DAVID: I . . . No. I just . . . This is maybe a cool opportunity, and I guess my preference would have been to have some . . . *time.*

BENJAMIN: You'll do great.

DAVID: If you say so.

BENJAMIN: Talk about that band you like.

DAVID: You liked them too!

BENJAMIN: He actually wants to use one of their songs over the end credits.

DAVID: So?

BENJAMIN: So: bond over that, or something.

DAVID: Great.

BENJAMIN: Oh, also, be funny.

DAVID: What?

BENJAMIN: Be funny. Show him that you're funny.

DAVID: You want me to . . . tell *jokes*, or—

BENJAMIN: Don't be ridiculous.

DAVID: I just don't really know—

BENJAMIN: I mean just as a general approach to the conversation. It might be good not to be super-serious about the book and the whole situation.

DAVID: Is this what you guys talked about for an hour before I got here?

BENJAMIN: Not really.

DAVID: He spent an hour just now explaining to you all the reasons he wants *you* to do it rather than your schmuck friend from when you were a teenager who's fresh out of grad school and has no credits.

BENJAMIN: Um. No.

DAVID: So what did you talk about?

BENJAMIN: Shh. Shh.

DAVID: What.

BENJAMIN: Just: here he comes.

(BENJAMIN *points . . . the lights shift . . .* DAVID *looks off in the direction he is pointing . . . there is the sound of sustained applause . . .)*

SCENE THREE

(Over the course of the next six months after Scene Two. A bookstore.)

*(*BENJAMIN *sits on a tall stool, at a podium, with a small clip-on microphone. He sips from a glass of water on the podium. The applause dies down.)*

BENJAMIN: Thanks. Thank you. And since the whole purpose of this, from the very beginning, was really just to *connect* with people . . . to see you all here is really . . . very meaningful. And I'm pretty nervous. I'm at the beginning of a long stretch of these, but this is only the second public reading I've done, and the first in a bookstore, which has a certain . . . I mean, an enormous corporate bookstore, but it's still *kind of* a bookstore . . . So. Thanks. *(Pause.)* Oh, uh, questions, questions. *(Pause.)* Uh . . . Anybody?

(Lights up on DAVID. *He sits at a desk, dialing a phone.)*

BENJAMIN: *(Pointing into the audience)* Yes. You.

DAVID: Hey, it's me. Um, congratulations on the *review*, that's . . . it's really exciting. I hope they're *all* that good. And, oh, oh, I saw the book! Like: the actual physical *object*, in a bookstore today, which . . . I mean: there it *was*. On the *shelf*. Between, you know, other authors, with . . . a jacket, and an author photo, and everything, and seeing that was really . . . I felt something. It was . . . very cool. *(Beat.)* Oh, and, I know it's your birthday tomorrow so, hey: happy . . . that. Twenty-five. You've still got time. So. Uh . . . Talk to you soon. Bye.

BENJAMIN: Well, first of all, let me say that, um: you're not exactly Methuselah yourself, young lady. But look: to articulate something in writing is a particular skill, like any other skill, but, you know, to make an observation, that might be the kind of thing a writer would write down . . . that's . . . *universal*. And that has nothing to do with *age*. So, in a way, my putting it down on the page and you . . . your lifting it up *off* the page . . . is sort of the same thing. *(Beat.)* Which, in a way, answers your question. *(He points.)* Um. Yes.

DAVID: What's up, dude? It's me. *Wow*, huh? I mean, I said I *hoped* they would all be that good, which, of course, was, you know, lip service, and who expected . . . Just . . . they're sort of . . . universally stellar. *(Beat.)* Oh, and it's weird to see "Benjamin" everywhere, like, it's just so hard not to think of you as *Ben*, but now it's *Benjamin*, so . . . that's just kind of, uh . . . *(Beat.)* Anyway, I wanted to start working on the screenplay, but after I typed up all of our notes from that meeting? And then turned them into a, uh, a treatment . . . which I'm sorry was, like, eighteen pages long, but, anyway, whatever: I kind of never heard anything back, like . . . at *all*. And so, you know, it's fine either way, but I basically just wanted to know how to proceed. *(Beat.) Anyway.* I would love to know how you're handling everything. Uh. Bye.

BENJAMIN: Well, I don't know what you mean by that. I mean: I have so many layers of protection, I am so . . . *removed* . . . from a person who might be in a magazine, or a newspaper, that I . . . It really doesn't feel like it's me. I mean, it's *not* me. *(He shrugs. Simply:)* It's not me. *(Beat.)* Uh. Yes. You. *(He points.)* You.

DAVID: Hey, Ben, it's, uh . . . it's me. I know that you're out of town, in, like, Scandinavia somewhere I think, at this point . . . Hope you're enjoying the, uh, fjords . . . and, you know, the Nordic chicks, so, uh . . . but I figure you've got to be checking these every now and then, so . . . I, uh . . . Oh, so I ran into your actor friend. At the opening of a play. And I, you know, made sure not to mention anything about the screenplay? And then he didn't either? But the thought of asking sort of made me feel like a . . . presumptuous jackass? Which is what I ended up feeling like anyway from talking to him at all? I don't know, I think maybe he's mad, or he didn't like me, because I argued with him about his ideas, like . . . *(Beat.)* But, I'm sorry, he wanted to end the movie with that incredibly cheesy line, like: "And now: the adventure begins." And, so, sure, I was just like, come *on*, it's not Disney, you know, it's not . . . *(Beat.)* Whatever, so: I have absolutely no idea what is going on. *(Beat.)* Sorry, just, you know. Call me. When you get back. Um. Okay. Bye.

BENJAMIN: Well, first of all, there's no need to apologize. Because your English is excellent. Um: I don't know what the next one is going to be. Frankly, I don't know that there'll *be* a next one. First of all, because I've been touring forever, and it's hard to imagine a time when I won't be, but, mainly . . . Just because people are now waiting for you to write something doesn't mean you have anything to write about. *(Beat.)* I mean, when I was *writing* the book . . . I wasn't necessarily planning to even *write* a book. Mainly, it was just . . . a pressure? Inside of me? To, I guess, to *make* something? Which is why all that stuff, that, you know, the reviews, I mean, all that stuff is . . . it's just . . . *nonsense.* If there's a next one, it'll be because there *needs* to be. And it will be what it needs to be. *(Pause.)* Yes. You.

DAVID: Hey, Benjamin, it's me. It's, uh, it's Dave. Actually, I don't even know if you're in town right now, but I am . . .

BENJAMIN: Um. What do you mean?

DAVID: But whatever, whatever, if you *are* around . . . which actually I think you are . . . Actually, I guess you *must* be, because I saw that you're reading next week here, so, you know, I guess you're going to be . . . physically present, at the, uh . . .

BENJAMIN: I don't understand.

DAVID: Anyway, I, uh, I started working on the screenplay. I guess . . . on, uh, "spec." As they say? Turns out, though, your actor friend decided to write it himself. In fact, he's about to start shooting it. Apparently.

BENJAMIN: I'm sorry?

DAVID: Yeah. It's just . . . something he mentioned. In an interview. That I read. *(Pause.)* I read it, man. *(Pause.)* Um. Okay.

BENJAMIN: I'm sorry. I don't understand the question.

DAVID: Wait, I feel like I'm forgetting something.

BENJAMIN: Yes. *(Pause.)* You.

(BENJAMIN points . . . the lights shift . . . DAVID goes off . . . BENJAMIN takes out a cigarette and lights it . . . the space changes around him . . .)

SCENE FOUR

(Five years before Scene Three. An apartment in Prague.)

(BENJAMIN is sitting at a desk, at a laptop computer, gazing out a window. He smokes, ashing into a mug on the table. There is a giant stuffed bear seated on the floor, leaning against a bed.)

(DAVID enters, bleary, in a T-shirt and boxers.)

DAVID: Hey.

BENJAMIN: Hey.

DAVID: How long have you been up?

BENJAMIN: A few hours. Since seven.

DAVID: Jesus. What is wrong with you?

BENJAMIN: I'm working.

DAVID: Yeah, that's not an answer.

BENJAMIN: Sleep is for the dead. Live your fucking life.

DAVID: Uh. Okay. Although I could say the same to you.

BENJAMIN: You could. But it would be misguided.

DAVID: Why?

BENJAMIN: Because I'm *working*.

DAVID: So am I!

BENJAMIN: Fine. So we're both working according to our own schedules.

DAVID: Right, but I'm not *only* working. Look, we're in Prague for the summer, I'm *working* at a *bar* so we get free drinks, and you're going to bed at ten every night. Live *your* fucking life.

BENJAMIN: I am.

DAVID: Well, one of us is going to have to switch. This sucks. There's like three hours in the middle of every day when we're both awake, so we hardly hang out at all.

BENJAMIN: So get *up* earlier.

DAVID: So fucking stay up *later*.

BENJAMIN: Well, we shouldn't do *both*.

DAVID: Right, no, maybe we should trade lives. We'll pray to a voodoo skull, and then, after a while, we'll each gain a more profound understanding of one another, and then, just when we're really settling in, we'll switch back.

BENJAMIN: Okay.

DAVID: Just . . . that would be, the, you know . . . the Disney version.

BENJAMIN: I'll take your word for it.

DAVID: Okay. *(Beat.)* What do you mean?

(Offstage, a door slams.)

BENJAMIN: What was that?

DAVID: The, uh . . . the door.

(Beat.)

BENJAMIN: Did you bring that girl back here last night?

DAVID: You didn't hear us come in?

BENJAMIN: No. Was that her leaving?

DAVID: I . . . believe so, yes.

BENJAMIN: You guys fool around?

DAVID: Well, yeah. I mean . . . yeah. It's like a twenty-five-minute walk back here from the bar. She didn't, you know, accompany me back here at three in the morning to, like, *see* the place.

BENJAMIN: *(In Indian accent)* "And this is the kitchen area . . . and these are our pots, and also pans . . ."

DAVID: Why am I Indian in this joke?

BENJAMIN: I . . . don't know.

DAVID: Yeah, just seemed kinda . . . arbitrary.

BENJAMIN: Okay. *(Pause.)* Did you have *sex* with her?

DAVID: I . . . *(Pause.)* Yes.

BENJAMIN: That is so lame.

DAVID: What?

BENJAMIN: That is just really lame.

DAVID: *Why?*

BENJAMIN: Because! Okay. Who are the people you've had sex with?

DAVID: What do you mean?

BENJAMIN: The others were, what, girlfriends, right?

DAVID: Right.

BENJAMIN: Girls who you were in *love* with. And now *this* random, like, British girl, who you will never see again, and whose *name* you don't even know.

DAVID: Her name is Susan.

BENJAMIN: Susan what?

(Pause.)

DAVID: She works at a museum.

BENJAMIN: I just think that's kind of lame, that's all.

DAVID: *You told me to do it!*

BENJAMIN: What are you talking about?

DAVID: Last night! We're at the bar? In that corner booth that's way too big for the two of us, so Susan and her friends ask if we mind if they join us, and then they slide in on the other side of it, and we bum cigarettes from them, and based on those, like, minuscule exchanges you lean over to me, point across the bar in the other direction, and say: "I'm pointing in the other direction so she won't know we're talking about her, but I think you could totally score with that British girl who just gave you a cigarette."

BENJAMIN: And?

DAVID: And then you said, "Just tap me on the leg if you want me to leave so you guys can be alone."

BENJAMIN: So?

DAVID: So then . . . and, by the way, let the record reflect that I never, ever tapped you on the leg . . . you got up and you left.

BENJAMIN: It was ten. What's your point?

DAVID: So why are you giving me *grief* about it *today*?

BENJAMIN: I didn't mean for you to have *sex* with her. That just . . . cheapens it.

DAVID: Cheapens what?

BENJAMIN: The whole . . . enterprise.

DAVID: Having sex with a girl cheapens the enterprise of bringing her home from a bar.

BENJAMIN: Look: I meant for you to have *intimacy*. But there are all kinds of ways to be intimate. And when it comes to touching things in ways that are kind of sacred . . . there's something to be said for touching only the sacred things.

DAVID: So I should have pursued a different *kind* of intimacy.

BENJAMIN: I guess.

DAVID: Like maybe a blow job.

BENJAMIN: We're having two totally different conversations.

DAVID: What conversation are *you* having?

BENJAMIN: Okay: I've been exchanging letters all summer with Emily. And I just know that I've found that, instead of staying out and looking for something . . . *else* . . . that I've preferred to come home to those.

DAVID: To the love letters.

BENJAMIN: Well: *all* letters are love letters. After all.

DAVID: I have no idea what you mean by that.

BENJAMIN: I just feel like it's . . . *better.*

DAVID: What is better than what?

BENJAMIN: It's *real.* You choose them, and they choose you, and that choice remains constant, if nobody is watching, or if everybody is watching. This other way, it's about *you* only, it's a kind of *performance,* and a kind of *accumulation,* and, at the same time, it's not even *really* the actual quality of *you* at *all,* because, for *them,* it's only about *them.* And while you have your tongues in each other's mouth, both of you are already thinking about how to tell the story to your friends the next day. That's not real.

DAVID: Then why doesn't it feel bad?

BENJAMIN: What do you mean?

DAVID: It feels great. And, yes, absolutely, I was totally excited to tell you about it today. There's this buoyancy in my stomach. I feel like I no longer have to worry about . . . *anything.* Which is totally disproportionate, I know, but it doesn't matter: that's how I feel. As opposed to having a girlfriend, which, in my actual experience, seems to make all of these things, which are supposed to be *fun,* instead be kind of fraught, except for, like, at the very beginning, so why not just have a series of very very *beginnings,* and if that isn't *better,* then why does it *feel* so much better?

BENJAMIN: Oh, well, everything that's not real feels better. Because you're not *risking* anything. So it will continue to feel better until you acknowledge that it's not real.

DAVID: Why would I want to do that?

BENJAMIN: What do you mean?

DAVID: If it's just going to make something that's a lot of fun feel worse.

BENJAMIN: Well, okay, I mean, why have sex at all? Masturbation is better.

DAVID: No it's not.

BENJAMIN: Sure it is. The only reason sex is better is because you can think to yourself: "Aww, yeah, I'm having sex."

DAVID: So the goal is to get to the point where I can derive contentment from thinking: "Aww, yeah, I'm having a relationship."

BENJAMIN: It might not be up to you. You may be *forced* to acknowledge that it's not real *because* it stops feeling better.

DAVID: When I grow up, you're saying.

BENJAMIN: I'm just telling you what I think.

DAVID: Fabulous.

BENJAMIN: You may think differently.

DAVID: I don't actually know what I think.

BENJAMIN: I mean, don't get upset. I don't want to get into a whole disagreement.

DAVID: Well, I was actually pretty psyched that this happened, and you're making me feel a little bad about it.

BENJAMIN: Well that wasn't my intention. *(Pause.)* So tell me about it.

DAVID: Pardon?

BENJAMIN: Tell me about it.

DAVID: I'm not gonna *tell* you about it.

BENJAMIN: You said you were excited to.

DAVID: Right, so, I guess you'd like to disapprove of my actions while also deriving from them a voyeuristic thrill.

BENJAMIN: Fine. Don't tell me.

*(*BENJAMIN *turns back to his computer and begins typing. Pause.)*

DAVID: I mean, it was very, very easy to talk to this girl.

*(*BENJAMIN *turns back.)*

BENJAMIN: Go on.

DAVID: Well, and this one thing especially was really kind of cool, which was that . . . and, I mean, never ever previously in my life have I not had to make the first move, I mean, to not have to actually do the leaning in and the kissing myself . . . I mean, I don't mean *always*, obviously, like not *within* an ongoing *relationship*, of course not, girls will initiate . . . things, but I mean the *very* first kiss with someone new, but with this girl . . . I was in, like, midsentence, and she leans in and kisses me. That has never happened to me before. And we just start making out. And then we left the bar, and, you know how all summer it's been so maddening to watch like eight dozen couples making out on the Charles Bridge every night, and wondering: "Where the hell are these people *finding* each other?"

BENJAMIN: I hadn't really noticed.

DAVID: Well, it's been maddening for me, maddening, so I made *sure* on the way home to cross the Charles Bridge and make out with her on it, like, *fuck you*, you fucking *backpackers*, and, don't get me wrong, it was really sweet, and, of *course* we're totally exoticizing each other, like the very *fact* of her accent is enough to make her attractive to me, though, I mean, *you* saw her, she was supercute.

BENJAMIN: Yeah. She was.

DAVID: And even though I kind of got the impression that she doesn't feel so good necessarily about where she is in her, I guess, *real* life, maybe careerwise, like she works in a museum and didn't sound very excited about it, but while she's here in Prague with her friends she could feel how, in my eyes, she's just this sort of dark-haired, dashing British girl. And it worked the other way, too. Because . . . and she *said* this to me at one point, she *said* this, and I thought it was just so sweet, she said: *(In British accent)* "You're the nicest American I've ever met." And I thought: Who has she met? Those . . . backpackers on the bridge. Those blond guys from football schools in Florida. And I felt . . . I was like, "Yeah. Yeah." I felt like: "I represent the very best qualities of my nation." The ones not in evidence in most of the, I guess, *ambassadors* we send out internationally, but here I am, sort of an anomaly, to say: "No. We are also like this." I felt . . . really proud. Oh, oh, and *this* was the coolest thing.

BENJAMIN: What.

DAVID: Well, because she works in a museum, she knows a lot about art, you know, about architecture, and I talked to her about my play that I'm working on?

BENJAMIN: Right. What's that about?

DAVID: Ruskin, uh, John Ruskin, and, but, so, you know, the architecture in this city is so gorgeous, and we're walking through the streets at night, on our way back here, and so we're talking about the buildings, and I talk to her all about . . . like, okay, how, like: the ability to make a, you know, a crenellated . . . whatever. Spandrel. As an ornament for a *building*. And how, like, a really good adult *craftsman* could make, you know, eighty *thousand* of those in a row that are all beautiful in exactly the same way, but some other part of you, the, like, child who knows nothing, is like: "Hey! Forget spandrels!" And, you know, shock and horror: "But we've been making crenellated spandrels for five hundred years!" But, no, like: "Screw *that*. What about, um . . . some acanthus leaves?" But, you know, then it's the craftsman in you that has to execute. Because maybe it *is* a good idea, but if you can't pull it off, you know, people will say, "See? Spandrels are the only way to go, just like we've always known." People will say, "Will you look at that stupid kid? Oh, well, he'll grow out of *that*." And it's like, "No. No. Please don't. Just give him time to learn how to *execute*." And how, Ruskin says, you sort of have to somehow combine those two mutually exclusive things, the craftsman and the child, to really . . . build good buildings. To have . . . both at once. That's . . . genius.

BENJAMIN: You're writing a *play* about this?

DAVID: Hey, it's *good*. I think it's really really good. Anyway, *she* was interested in *all* of it.

BENJAMIN: She wanted to sleep with you.

DAVID: Well, yeah. And when we got to the front door of the apartment building, she said: "Do you have condoms?" And I said: "Hey. I grew up in California." And she said: "I have no idea what that means." So I was just, like: "Yes. Yes I do."

(Pause.)

BENJAMIN: That's an incredibly, incredibly boring story.

DAVID: Fuck you.

BENJAMIN: Anything that might come out of your mouth from this day forward, be it a belch or spittle, would be of more interest than that story.

DAVID: Why do you have to be such a dick?

(DAVID leaves.)

BENJAMIN: Come on! *(Pause.)* Come on! Stop being such a baby!

(DAVID comes back.)

DAVID: What?

BENJAMIN: What did you *do*?

DAVID: What do you want from me? We had sex.

BENJAMIN: How?

DAVID: I . . . *How?* Do you, like, need a tutorial?

BENJAMIN: Were you on top? Was *she* on top?

DAVID: I . . . no. What do you . . . ? *(Beat.)* We did it from behind.

BENJAMIN: Why are you so uncomfortable?

DAVID: I'm not uncomfortable.

BENJAMIN: You seem pretty uncomfortable.

DAVID: I'm not.

BENJAMIN: So . . . she had sex with you from behind. *(Off* DAVID's *look)* I'm totally kidding. I know you don't do that. Anymore.

DAVID: *(Starting to leave)* Dude, if you're gonna be like this—

BENJAMIN: What is wrong with you? Why are you all defensive?

DAVID: I just feel like you're being kind of an asshole.

BENJAMIN: Okay, okay.

(BENJAMIN goes over to the bed, grabs the oversized stuffed bear, places it on all fours, and kneels behind it.)

DAVID: What are you doing?

BENJAMIN: So you're behind her.

DAVID: Stop that. *(Pause.)* Yes.

BENJAMIN: How did you get her to do that?

DAVID: What?

BENJAMIN: I just mean . . . with someone you don't know very well, it's not usually the first thing you go to.

DAVID: Oh, uh . . . It, uh, it was kind of a misunderstanding, actually.

BENJAMIN: Pardon?

DAVID: We were kissing and whatever, and I was on top of her, and I was—

(BENJAMIN flips the bear over, into missionary position.)

BENJAMIN: Like this.

DAVID: That's very disconcerting. But, yes, and I was *trying* to get her to roll over on top of me, you know, shifting so we're both kind of on our sides, and then trying to get her to throw her leg over my hip. Right? So that if I rolled onto my back, she'd sort of end up straddling me.

(BENJAMIN demonstrates this maneuver with the bear.)

BENJAMIN: Like so.

DAVID: But instead I think she actually misunderstood what I was trying to do, like, I had my hand on the back of her thigh and I was sort of gently lifting her leg toward the eventual destination of my hip, but I guess she thought I was trying to turn her over completely . . . so she did.

BENJAMIN: She did.

DAVID: Just . . . hopped onto all fours.

(BENJAMIN returns the bear to all fours.)

BENJAMIN: Thusly.

DAVID: Yeah.

BENJAMIN: And you were like: *(He sings)* "It's beginning to look a lot like Christmas . . ."

DAVID: Yeah, okay, could you stop fucking the bear now?

BENJAMIN: Hey, you ever try it like this?

(BENJAMIN flips onto his back and has the bear straddle him, backward)

DAVID: Yes, I believe that's called the "reverse cowgirl."

BENJAMIN: It's pretty great. Because, one, we get to see everything, which we love, and, two, she's got this great angle for a kind of thrusting action, which really allows her to—

DAVID: *Please leave the bear alone.*

BENJAMIN: What's your problem?

DAVID: I . . . ! *(Beat.) We're subletting!*

BENJAMIN: I know that.

DAVID: I just . . . It's not your bear.

BENJAMIN: Okay.

(DAVID *grabs the bear and carries it off.* BENJAMIN *returns to his desk and lights another cigarette.* DAVID *returns.)*

DAVID: The bear probably needs one, too, now.

BENJAMIN: No, the bear's trying to quit. She told me.

DAVID: Can I have one?

BENJAMIN: Take mine.

*(*BENJAMIN *gives the cigarette to* DAVID.)

BENJAMIN: So . . . How was it?

DAVID: Physically? Kind of awkward and brief. Psychologically? Amazing.

BENJAMIN: Well, you're very fortunate, I guess.

(Pause.)

DAVID: You're jealous.

BENJAMIN: Um. What?

DAVID: No, it's okay, I just got it.

BENJAMIN: I'm jealous.

DAVID: Yes. That's the source of your sudden, nonsensically puritanical stance. It's envy.

BENJAMIN: If you say so.

DAVID: I do say so.

BENJAMIN: You may be right.

DAVID: I think I am.

BENJAMIN: Maybe so.

DAVID: This may be a first.

BENJAMIN: What do you mean?

DAVID: This may be the first time I have witnessed active, palpable envy of me emanating from you.

BENJAMIN: I'm sure that's not true.

DAVID: Oh no, don't get me wrong, not you, like, *exceed* me in all things, or whatever, just, mainly, because envy is kind of not your style, you have this remarkable self-possession, it's one of the things that make you a seductive friend, you rarely seem to *need* anything. From outside yourself.

BENJAMIN: What are you talking about?

DAVID: Well, for example: it is impossible for me to imagine you making a similarly detailed observation about me.

BENJAMIN: Certainly not to your face.

DAVID: I mean that it doesn't seem like you look to others to guide your behavior. To compare yourself. I admire that.

BENJAMIN: Thank you. I think.

DAVID: Except in this case, when you're consumed with envy.

BENJAMIN: Okay.

DAVID: I'm not making a big deal about it. I'm just saying: this is a momentously historic occasion that must be enshrined for all time.

(DAVID goes.)

BENJAMIN: What are you doing?

(BENJAMIN turns back to his computer and continues to type. DAVID returns with a camera.)

BENJAMIN: Oh, come on—

DAVID: Look defeated.

BENJAMIN: Uh . . . Can't help it.

DAVID: And by the way, okay, here's what I think.

BENJAMIN: About what?

DAVID: I think that it's just as safe to keep calling back your girlfriend as it is *not* to call back your one-night stand. So it's not as if *your* way doesn't have exactly the same problem. You're still just as afraid of taking a risk. Not because you're being intimate in a certain way, or in another certain way, but because you're being intimate . . . at all.

BENJAMIN: Maybe so.

DAVID: And you know what I *really* want is to have both. Like: a girlfriend who is, every single day, a total stranger. Or, like, a random pickup, who I'm with for only a day but who knows me better than anybody in the world. I want to have both at once. Which I'm a little bit afraid is impossible.

BENJAMIN: Everything worth doing is impossible.

(DAVID lifts the camera and takes the photo . . . there is a series of flashes . . . the lights shift . . . BENJAMIN goes . . . the space changes around DAVID . . . flickering light . . .)

SCENE FIVE

(Sometime after Scene Three.)

(A movie premiere. BENJAMIN *stands in a pool of flickering light created by the flashes of hundreds of paparazzi cameras . . . he goes off . . .)*

(A movie theater. DAVID *sits alone. Flickering light from a movie in progress plays across his face. A movie sound track underscores whatever action he is watching.* DAVID *eats popcorn. We hear a voice, dialogue from the screen: "And now: the adventure begins."* DAVID *reacts. The sound track music subsides. A song begins, something moody and evocative by a very indy band.* DAVID *reacts . . . the song plays . . . the space changes around him . . .)*

SCENE SIX

*(A little over a year after Scene Four. A college dorm room. The song contin-
ues, now playing from a stereo in the room.* BENJAMIN *sits at his desk.*
DAVID *sits on the floor with his back against the bed.)*

BENJAMIN: What party?

DAVID: The, uh, the one that girl told us about?

BENJAMIN: What girl?

DAVID: The, uh . . . the girl in your fiction-writing seminar?

BENJAMIN: Oh. From Celeste's class?

DAVID: I . . . Yes, from "Celeste's" class.

BENJAMIN: Jessica.

DAVID: Yes. Right.

BENJAMIN: Oh. Uh. *(Pause.)* Why?

DAVID: I don't know. Because she made a point of telling us about it. *(Beat.)* Although, hey, not very memorably, obviously, so—

BENJAMIN: *(Overlapping)* No, no, I remember. I just . . . It's not a party. She said it was just a small gathering of like a handful of people in her room.

DAVID: I know she did.

BENJAMIN: Ah. Well . . .

DAVID: What.

BENJAMIN: Well, first of all, you have a *girlfriend,* so—

DAVID: I don't want to *nail* anybody, dude. I just, I'm away from school, and I want to go out, and have a good time, and, like, flirt.

BENJAMIN: And anyway—

DAVID: *What.*

BENJAMIN: I don't . . . care for her. Particularly. *Or* her friends.

DAVID: Dude: she is *really* cute. I mean: what is she? I mean: racially. She's, I guess, Asian, but, like . . . partly, or—

BENJAMIN: Her mother is Japanese and her father is Caribbean.

DAVID: You've discussed this with her.

BENJAMIN: Um: it's all she fucking writes about.

DAVID: You find that annoying.

BENJAMIN: Extraordinarily.

DAVID: She seems okay to me.

BENJAMIN: No she doesn't.

DAVID: She doesn't seem okay to me?

BENJAMIN: She *shouldn't*.

DAVID: What's wrong with her?

BENJAMIN: I don't know. You heard her.

DAVID: I heard her what.

BENJAMIN: Um. Talking?

DAVID: What do you mean?

BENJAMIN: Okay. Case in point. She said: "I want to be a novelist."

DAVID: So?

BENJAMIN: She says that *all the time*.

DAVID: So? It's a fiction-writing seminar.

BENJAMIN: So what a strange, strange thing to say! She doesn't know what it *means*.

DAVID: Neither do you.

BENJAMIN: Yes, but I have never, ever once in my life ever *said* that. That's the *point*. Of *course* I don't know what it means. You know? All these girls . . . and it *is* usually girls . . . *(Beat.)* I mean, don't *quote* me on this, this particular observation is not to leave this room, but . . . Okay, you've taken fiction-writing seminars at school, right?

DAVID: Yeah. A few.

BENJAMIN: Is it like ninety-nine percent girls there too?

DAVID: That is one of the reasons I continue to take them.

BENJAMIN: They sit there, in their cat-eye glasses, dressed in black like they're mourning the fact that they have nothing to actually *mourn*, except, you know, that's great that you were bulimic when you were fifteen, but I'm really not interested in *reading* about it. *(Beat.)* And they all want to go to *graduate* school. For master's degrees in *writing*. And I'm just like: *why?*

DAVID: Uh . . .

BENJAMIN: You know?

DAVID: I . . . Sure.

BENJAMIN: What.

DAVID: No, I . . .

BENJAMIN: What.

DAVID: Nothing. *(Pause.)* I'm applying to grad school.

BENJAMIN: For *what?*

DAVID: What do you mean "for what"? For playwriting.

BENJAMIN: I mean what for?

DAVID: What?

BENJAMIN: Why?

DAVID: Why . . . what? I . . . because . . . that's what people . . . do next . . . ?

BENJAMIN: What people?

DAVID: Um. Budding . . . playwrights? So that . . . you'll be taken more seriously? I don't know. Look: what's your point?

BENJAMIN: Originally, my point was that we should skip this stupid fucking party, but we seem to have strayed.

DAVID: To *what*?

BENJAMIN: Nothing. Just: I would *never* consider going to graduate school.

DAVID: Well, it's different, okay? Theater is different.

BENJAMIN: How is it different?

DAVID: It's *collaborative*. You have to learn how to *use* that. And also then you have that sort of stamp of approval from having gone to a grad school and that lets people know your work is maybe worth paying attention to.

BENJAMIN: Won't that depend on whether or not your work is good?

DAVID: Well, that's assuming they read it, which, without some indication it's going to be worth their time, they maybe *won't*.

BENJAMIN: And then what?

DAVID: *Then* maybe an agent will look at your work. And then *he* can get *theaters* to read it.

BENJAMIN: And then what?

DAVID: *Then* . . . an audience gets to see it.

BENJAMIN: Why can't you just take some friends of yours who are actors and direct them in your play and invite an audience?

DAVID: Because . . .

BENJAMIN: Because what?

DAVID: Because that would not satisfy my ego. Obviously.

BENJAMIN: Look, all I'm saying is: *I* think the thing to be afraid of is not that you will never publish, or whatever, but that *you will never write anything good.* And I think if I *did* write something good, if I *knew* that I had *done* that, I would be satisfied to let it just sit in a *drawer* forever. And I think that if that's not true, then the things I write probably won't be any good anyway. So, you know: why don't you maybe just start trying *that* for a while?

DAVID: I don't know!

BENJAMIN: Well . . . *(Beat.)* But, look, I don't want to get into a whole disagreement about it, I mean, I'm just asking.

DAVID: No, I know, it's a good question. *(Pause.)* I don't know.

BENJAMIN: You don't know what?

DAVID: I don't know what I don't know. *(Pause.)* Wow, you *really* don't want me to go flirt with this girl.

BENJAMIN: Whatever, I don't care.

DAVID: No, just, you're being awfully mean to me, when that is, like, the exact opposite of what I need right now. Jesus.

(Beat.)

BENJAMIN: What are you talking about?

DAVID: No, never mind, nothing, just . . . Whatever. Great. Jessica sucks. I hate her. Let's all just sit in this room and hate her together and have a big hate party where we masturbate over our hatred of her. That will be fantastic.

BENJAMIN: Is everything okay?

DAVID: Um. Why do you ask?

BENJAMIN: Because you're kind of losing your mind. Seriously, are you all right?

DAVID: Uh. I don't know. *(Pause.)* I don't know. *(Pause.)* I don't even really know how to talk about it.

BENJAMIN: We don't have to talk about it.

DAVID: Okay. *(Long pause.)* So, right, like you said, I've been seeing this girl.

BENJAMIN: Yeah.

DAVID: I don't know. Here's the thing. Here's what's so weird, is, it happened this one night, in this one *moment*, really, it . . . uh . . .

BENJAMIN: What happened?

DAVID: Okay. We're lying in bed together, you know . . . after . . . and we're going to sleep, and I just have this thought, this one, stray, like, rogue, thought, just creeps in, just sort of flits across my brain, and the thought is: What if I feel absolutely nothing for this person?

BENJAMIN: Huh.

DAVID: That was it. That was the thought. What if I feel nothing? And suddenly. I mean. It was like my heart . . . stopped. Or like I fell through ice. Or like. If my life was a movie? Like I was the hero, and I had *won*, I got the girl, you know, and the credits rolled, and, but, instead of it being over, and me being allowed to get up and, you know, *leave*, instead I was still stuck in the movie, and, even worse, everybody around me still believed the movie was real, and was still in character, and I had to, like, play along, but with no actual sentiment behind it, I mean, seriously, I just wanted to turn to her right there, in the dark, and say, "Hey. Remember when I said I loved you? What a great scene *that* was. Okay! That's a wrap! Maybe we'll work together again someday!" Only I can't do that. I mean: obviously. I mean: I don't want to *want* to. Because until like a second before that, literally like a second before, everything felt so . . . good. Just . . . fine. And then I have this one thought and everything just, like, inverted, like a photo negative, or . . . And not just with this girl, but suddenly I started seeing everything this way. From that moment. I, literally, I have been literally dividing my life, you know, mentally, into the moment before I had that thought and the moment after I had that thought. This one . . . *thought.* And I . . .

BENJAMIN: Uh . . .

DAVID: What.

BENJAMIN: Why don't you just break up with her?

DAVID: What?

BENJAMIN: It just . . . I mean: why don't you just break up with her?

DAVID: Are you even *listening* to me?

BENJAMIN: Yes.

DAVID: This . . . Because! This has gone like so far *beyond* that question, it's like tapped into this well of despair that I didn't even know was *in* there, and, so, what, great, I'll break up with her, and then I'll still feel this way about everything *else, and* I'll be alone, and then she'll date somebody else, and *that* will drive me crazy, and I just . . . no, no, that just seems worse.

BENJAMIN: So what do you *want*?

DAVID: What I *want* is to . . . go back to how it *was.* To feel how I felt a while ago about her and about *everything* I want to . . . undo . . . whatever has taken place and not ever ever ever feel this way again.

BENJAMIN: Uhh . . .

DAVID: What.

BENJAMIN: I mean . . .

DAVID: What. Say it.

BENJAMIN: It doesn't sound like the kind of thing you're going to be able to undo. Uh. Maybe ever. I mean, it *sounds* like it's just . . . a new thing you know about yourself. Which is probably not what you wanted to hear. But it may not actually be a bad thing either necessarily.

DAVID: How is it not a bad thing?

BENJAMIN: I don't know. Let's find out.

DAVID: What the hell does that mean?

BENJAMIN: Well. You clearly haven't found the good in it yet. So. Let's find out.

DAVID: Okay.

BENJAMIN: In the meantime, do you want some weed?

DAVID: Okay. *(Pause.)* Didn't you wonder what I was doing here?

BENJAMIN: No. I . . . assumed. That you just wanted to come visit.

DAVID: Well, of course. I mean. That too.

(BENJAMIN has by now taken a partially smoked joint out of his desk. He lights it. They pass the joint back and forth. And listen to the music. For a while.)

DAVID: How do you always do this?

BENJAMIN: Do what?

DAVID: Like: find a band that's really good but that almost nobody else likes yet. My whole life I can never be that guy. The guy who can be like: "Oh, man, of course I know that band, I liked them before they were huge." How do you do that?

BENJAMIN: I just . . . find music I like.

DAVID: Why didn't *I* think of that.

BENJAMIN: Heh. Right.

DAVID: Actually, no. Really. I mean, really. I mean. When I buy music? My first thought, like, the thing at the *forefront* of my mind, is who might *hear* it. I mean, like, *other* than me. The guys on my hall, if they'll hear me listening, or if I bring a girl home, if it would be something that would be good to maybe . . . I have a hard time . . .

BENJAMIN: What.

DAVID: I have a hard time doing things . . . ? Feeling that they're real, or that they *mean* anything? If nobody's watching.

BENJAMIN: Huh.

DAVID: You don't have that problem.

BENJAMIN: I think that everybody has that problem.

DAVID: But it doesn't stop you from actually doing things.

BENJAMIN: Oh, well, in that sense, no. I don't have that problem.

DAVID: But, see, *then* you totally squander it, you don't, like, lord it over other people to make them feel envious and inferior.

BENJAMIN: Why?

DAVID: Because you knew about the band first!

BENJAMIN: Oh. Well, I didn't. I mean, some record executive obviously already knew about it first, because it's in stores all over the country.

DAVID: Well, independent stores.

BENJAMIN: So?

DAVID: No, you're right, you're right, so I guess the only way you can really do it is if you were sitting in a basement one day, with the guys who would later be in the band, and then one of them was like, "Hey! We should form a band!" And they picked up instruments and started messing around, and then you were like: "Huh, it's rough, it's raw, but damn if I don't see the, like, seedlings of something really major happening here." *(Beat.)* But, see, then you're fucked anyway, because when they do make it, what *was* this private truth instead becomes this, like, obnoxious public *mythology* from which you, by necessity, because you are not actually *in* the band, are more or less *excised*, and so they'll be like, they'll be talking to a journalist, and be like, "Yeah, thanks to all the folks who believed in us in the beginning." And you're like: "Fuck you! I bought you your first pick! And now you're gonna sit there on the cover of the, like, local arts pull-out section of our hometown paper, posing on a bunch of fucking, like, giant concrete tubes at a construction site, when you and I *both* know you *never* worked construction—"

BENJAMIN: Hey, can I show you something?

DAVID: Uh. Yeah. What.

(BENJAMIN raises an eyebrow. Then he goes to his desk, opens a drawer, and pulls out a manuscript. He tosses it to DAVID.)

DAVID: What the hell is this? *(Beat.)* Hey!

BENJAMIN: Yeah.

DAVID: When did you finish it?

BENJAMIN: Just, like, a couple of weeks ago.

DAVID: Oh my God. It's *done.*

BENJAMIN: Well. A draft, yeah.

DAVID: Oh my God. *(Beat.)* Has anybody *read* it yet?

BENJAMIN: No. Well, Celeste. Actually, she wants to meet about it sometime next week. Which I'm actually sort of dreading, but . . . Yeah, no, that's it.

DAVID: Huh. Wow. *Wow. (Beat.)* You know what we should do?!

BENJAMIN: What.

DAVID: We should totally make a deal. As, like, a vote of confidence.

BENJAMIN: A deal about what?

DAVID: You sell your first novel, I take you out to lunch. And I get my first professional production, you take me out.

BENJAMIN: I . . . Okay, sure. I mean: that's a nice sentiment. It's nice.

DAVID: Okay. *(Pause.)* What kind of food do you want?

BENJAMIN: What do you mean?

DAVID: For your lunch!

BENJAMIN: I . . . What?

DAVID: When I take you out!

BENJAMIN: You want to . . . decide *now*? *(Pause.)* Uh . . . Indian?

DAVID: Done. I want Japanese-Caribbean fusion.

BENJAMIN: Ha-ha.

DAVID: So it's a deal?

BENJAMIN: Sure.

DAVID: Okay. *(Pause.)* I think it was true. What you said.

BENJAMIN: What I said when?

DAVID: About us going to different colleges. I think you were right.

BENJAMIN: Of course I was right. *(Pause.)* Hey. You're going to be *fine.* You're going to be totally *fine.* You know that, right?

DAVID: No. But thanks. And, I mean, if you're ever having, you know, girl problems, or whatever, and you need someone to . . . I mean, obviously, I'm there, okay? I'll be there.

BENJAMIN: Well, that's . . . *(Beat.)* Oh my God!

DAVID: What, what, what!

BENJAMIN: No, just: you have to hear this next track. It is *amazing.*

(Pause.)

DAVID: Okay.

BENJAMIN: It's from this live show they did. That I was *at.*

DAVID: Oh, yes, of *course* you were.

BENJAMIN: Shh. Shh. Here. Listen.

(BENJAMIN turns up the stereo . . . there is the sound of recorded audience murmuring . . . the space changes around them . . .)

SCENE SEVEN

(Two years after Scene Six. BENJAMIN *sits at a desk, dialing a phone.)*

BENJAMIN: Hey, it's me. Uh, so we . . . so my agent sent the book
to a publisher. Me and my, uh . . . Celeste's agent. So we're kind
of just waiting to hear, but, you know: it's out there now. So.
Yeah. Uh. Talk to you soon.

(Two and a half years later. DAVID, *on a stool, facing the audience.)*

DAVID: Thanks. Thank you so much. I, uh . . . Honestly, before I
came here I had no idea what to expect, I didn't really even have
an image in my mind of, um: Indiana. But I feel very . . . welcome. So thanks. *(Pause.)* Um. So, yeah, questions about anything,
about the play, or . . . You know, don't be shy, or I'm just going
to have to go to the, uh, to the movies. So. Yeah. *(Pointing into the
audience.)* Yes. You.

BENJAMIN: Hi, uh, so they turned it down. They, uh . . . You know,
it was a really positive response, a very kind rejection, though it's

still, in the end, a no. So we're moving on to the next place, I guess. I'll let you know what happens. Uh. Talk to you soon.

DAVID: Yes, I read them. I did read them. Um . . . I mean, what do you think? I found them . . . paralyzing and demoralizing. And I sort of understand why a lot of people say they won't ever even, uh . . . But, but, you know, this is hard work, it's supposed to be hard work, so, so, this idea that it sort of just emerges perfectly formed, is, uh, it's nonsense. I'm still . . . I'm the first to acknowledge that there's work to be done. *(Pause.)* Uh. *(He points.)* Yes. You.

BENJAMIN: Hi, Dave, it's Ben. Um. So two for two. On rejections. But, just, uh . . . Are you even in town? I'm starting to remember now that maybe you're not, but I cannot for the life of me think of where you might be, so . . . uh . . . But anyway: Call me. I think it may just be time to . . . *(Pause.)* You know. Whatever, I'm just rambling and filling up your tape now, so . . . Call me.

DAVID: Well, I guess because the subject matter, uh . . . interested me, it captured . . . and so, sure, it involves *research*, and a kind of . . . heady conceit, that makes it kind of . . . remote from . . . And, I mean, sure, you can avoid the problem by simply writing from your own . . . experience. But I don't know that anything has happened in my life that merits a play.

BENJAMIN: David, you fucking cunt idiot, where the fuck are you? It's Ben. It's about . . . ten o'clock. And you should be home, because I want to talk to you, and the world ought to . . . adjust itself to my . . . whims. But you're probably out fucking your girlfriend. But so call me back. And we'll talk soon. Or, if not, we knew each other once. And that meant something. *(Pause.)* Oh, yeah, by the way: I left . . . my agent.

DAVID: Okay, let's be honest here, I mean, it's not exactly like the people writing those reviews know what the fuck they're talking about, okay? I mean, you can write with a, like, faux-British inflection, and wear a bow tie all you want, you're still a critic for some tiny paper in Indiana, okay? I mean, no disrespect, I just mean: okay: please stop using my *biography* as an excuse not to pay attention to what I actually *wrote*. Yeah, I'm young. So what's wrong with my play? It's *young*. Why? Because that is the *safest fucking thing you can possibly say*. And so you'll do the safe thing. Because you're lazy. And you're a coward.

(BENJAMIN's phone rings. He answers it.)

BENJAMIN: Hello?

(During the following, BENJAMIN *talks quietly, makes notes on a notepad.)*

DAVID: Because *then*, as soon as it's *safe*: everybody comes out of the woodwork to praise you! Right when it doesn't *mean* anything! Brilliant, a tour de force, *now* youth is somehow this great *selling* point, *now* it makes the work *vibrant* and *clear-eyed*, it's *only possible* for someone so gloriously *young*, right? *No*. You're *still* lazy. You're *still* a coward. Risk something, motherfucker! *Risk* something!

BENJAMIN: Before you say anything else? This is starting to make me uncomfortable.

DAVID: *(He looks to one side.)* Oh, I'm making my director uncomfortable. He's perfectly comfortable with the reviews, however. Because they have no problem with him. Which is odd. Because he's a fucking charlatan. You're a *fraud*. You're *faking* it because you can get *away* with it. With terrible actors on an awful set under crappy lights, I mean, Jesus, my words have to run this, like, gauntlet of morons, before anybody gets to *hear* them, and that's somehow *my* fault?

*(*BENJAMIN *hangs up and goes off.)*

DAVID: Where are you going? Oh, did I hurt your feelings? Was it *painful* to be *exposed* in front of an *audience*? Well, there's a first time for everything. Fucker. Get off my stage. I hate you. That is so totally appropriate that you should leave me alone up here because that's the way I feel *already. (Beat.)* Any other questions? Yeah. I'm just *bitter*, right? Well, big fucking surprise. I mean: *this is supposed to be fun. Not*, uh, uhhh: excruciating! You know what the first sign is that an event is bad for a writer? You have to wear a *suit* to it. Swanky opening night? Bad. Award ceremony? Bad. The fact that I need an *agent*, some guy to be in a suit *for* me, and watch over the scruffy kid in me, and, like, protect me from getting *screwed*, the fact that I even *need* that: don't you see that that's *killing* us? That that's turning us into *cynics*? This is not why I started doing this. This is . . . I just . . . I just want . . . I want . . . *(Then, quietly)* Why don't you . . . *risk* something? *(Beat.)* Get out. All of you. Get out. Get the fuck *out*.

*(*DAVID *goes.* BENJAMIN *comes back. He makes a call.)*

BENJAMIN: Hey, Dave. It's Benjamin. I, uh, sorry I uh . . . You know what? I'm fine. Actually, I'm very fine. Actually, uh, technically . . . you owe me lunch. At, uh, at, if I recall correctly, at an Indian place. So. Uh. Call me. When you get a chance.

*(*BENJAMIN *hangs up and goes off . . . the space changes . . .)*

SCENE EIGHT

(*A year and a half later. A theater lobby. A row of double doors lead into the house, and a sign hangs from each reading:* QUIET PLEASE. PERFORMANCE IN PROGRESS.)

(DAVID *stands in the lobby, wearing a suit, holding one door slightly ajar, his head poked inside. Sounds of an audience, and a bit of stage light, spill out. Laughter. A cough. We hear a few lines of dialogue spoken, distantly, from the stage within: "Get out. All of you. Get out. Get the fuck out." As the final answering machine message begins,* DAVID *closes the door and turns away from it. He paces nervously. He takes out a cigarette.*)

(*Another door from the house opens.* BENJAMIN *walks out, heading for the exit.* DAVID *is at the other end of the lobby, and* BENJAMIN *does not notice him until, just before he reaches the exit, he hears* DAVID *speak.*)

DAVID: Hey.

(BENJAMIN *turns.*)

BENJAMIN: Hey.

(Pause.)

DAVID: Uh. Heading out for a smoke?

BENJAMIN: No. *(Pause.)* I quit. Actually.

DAVID: Oh.

BENJAMIN: So. Uh. Good to see you.

*(*BENJAMIN *turns to go.)*

DAVID: Where the hell are you going?

BENJAMIN: *(He turns back.)* I, uh . . . *(Pause.)* Home?

DAVID: You're not gonna talk to me?

BENJAMIN: What do you mean?

DAVID: Well, you're clearly *upset*, I mean—

BENJAMIN: I'm not, I'm not upset.

DAVID: You're walking out of my play.

BENJAMIN: I, uh . . . Well . . . *(Pause.)* I didn't know you were here tonight.

(Beat.)

DAVID: What?

BENJAMIN: Just . . .

DAVID: It's previews. I'm here every night.

BENJAMIN: Yeah, well, me too. Apparently.

DAVID: See? You're upset.

BENJAMIN: No I'm not.

DAVID: Just tell me. *Tell* me that you're upset.

BENJAMIN: I'm *not upset.*

DAVID: Then why are you leaving?

BENJAMIN: I just . . . I'm . . .

DAVID: *(Overlapping)* You're upset. You're leaving because you're upset.

BENJAMIN: *(Overlapping)* I'm not. I'm just . . . *leaving,* I'm not upset.

DAVID: *Yes you are.*

BENJAMIN: *Well, how the fuck would you feel? (Pause.)* Yes. I'm upset.

DAVID: Okay. *(Pause.)* Why?

BENJAMIN: What?

DAVID: Tell me why.

BENJAMIN: Um. Because I come off like a self-satisfied, pretentious asshole?

DAVID: Really?

BENJAMIN: Yes, *really.*

DAVID: Because *I* think he comes off pretty well.

BENJAMIN: Are you kidding? "Touch only the sacred things"? "Everything worth doing is impossible"? Who *talks* like that?

DAVID: You, kind of. Anyway, the audiences at all the workshops—

BENJAMIN: Oh, wonderful.

DAVID: No, they liked him *more*. Well, no, that's not true. They actually hated them both. But *I* think he's by far the more likable of the two. I think . . . the *other* one . . . comes off like a kind of needy cipher with no confidence in his own goals or ideals. *(Pause.)* Anyway, nobody knows it's you.

BENJAMIN: Of *course* they do.

DAVID: They don't. And if they don't see you making a *scene* in the *lobby*, they will continue not to know.

BENJAMIN: I was *leaving*. You're the one making it into a "scene."

DAVID: And, anyway, look, obviously, in a way, they're both *me*, okay? I'm a needy, pretentious, self-satisfied cipher asshole. I'm *both* of them.

BENJAMIN: Um. Okay. Back on *earth*: you know why I'm here? My *agent* called me. She read . . . something . . . somewhere. She called me, and she said, "I think someone wrote a play about you." Of *course* people know it's me.

DAVID: You're here because your *agent* called you?

BENJAMIN: What?

DAVID: I have a play in New York and you're here because your agent *called* you? And, incidentally: "someone"?

BENJAMIN: What.

DAVID: "I think *someone* wrote a play about you."

BENJAMIN: Oh, come on—

DAVID: We've known each other *ten years*, and your agent is unable to recognize my name.

BENJAMIN: *Who cares!? How* could you *write* about me?

DAVID: *How could you not write about me?*

(Pause.)

BENJAMIN: What does *that* mean?

DAVID: I mean . . . I feel like I *imagined* it.

BENJAMIN: What.

DAVID: Our *friendship*. I feel like I made it up, like it's just a bunch of stuff I manu*fac*tured in my *brain*, that I . . . *(Pause.)* I mean: *you're* half the reason I even *started* to . . . Do you even *know* that? *(Pause.)* So yes, maybe I was hoping we could have this *scene*, because *this* one I *did* imagine. So maybe I thought that if I could make it happen for real, then I would be allowed to think the rest of it was real, too. And obviously, you know, it was *necessary*, because you were gonna leave, you were totally just gonna leave without *talking* to me.

BENJAMIN: Well, we're talking now. So what did you imagine would happen?

DAVID: You know, in fact, it really wasn't something I could picture you actually taking part in.

BENJAMIN: So what did you think *you* would do?

DAVID: I don't *know*. That I'd . . . that I'd get to *tell* you . . .

BENJAMIN: What.

DAVID: You made me feel like crap.

(Pause.)

BENJAMIN: Okay. Is that all?

DAVID: Well. I guess . . . Yes. That's all.

BENJAMIN: Okay. *(Pause.)* I'm sorry.

DAVID: Good.

BENJAMIN: I definitely didn't mean to make you feel like crap.

DAVID: I *know* that. I *know* that. But what you don't get is that that's, like, *extra* infuriating! Because it didn't *occur* to you, even. There was no malice. You're not a malicious person. There was no *intent.* And the fact that it didn't occur to you is, itself, infuriating, because it's just . . . It was just so . . . indifferent. *(Pause.)* I mean, I think this is the first time that I've ever actually pissed you off.

BENJAMIN: Uh, that's not true.

DAVID: You know what I mean.

BENJAMIN: I don't, actually. We disagree all the time.

DAVID: Sure, but *I'm* the only one who gets worked up. You don't get upset at *me.* You just remain . . . placid. Asking *questions.* Trying to *understand.*

BENJAMIN: So what?

DAVID: So . . . nothing. This is a new experience. It's kind of . . . gratifying, that's all.

BENJAMIN: I just . . . don't like conflict. I don't see many good reasons to fight.

DAVID: Yeah, well, that's great, but sometimes it makes you come off like you just don't give a shit.

BENJAMIN: *(Snapping a little)* You know, if I'm such a bad friend, then maybe what's weird is that you *put up* with it for so long! Having some *idea* of me that fulfilled some *need* or *agenda* of *yours.*

I mean, have you considered the possibility that this is maybe, in the end, more *your* issue than it is mine?

DAVID: Yes. Of course I have.

BENJAMIN: And what did you conclude?

DAVID: That, to some extent . . . to some perhaps quite large extent . . . that that was probably the case.

BENJAMIN: Well, maybe you should have thought about that before you wrote a *play*.

DAVID: Dude. I *did* think about it.

BENJAMIN: Really.

DAVID: Yes.

BENJAMIN: And what happened?

DAVID: I wrote a play.

(Pause.)

BENJAMIN: Oh.

DAVID: I mean, just for *me*, at first. Initially, just for myself.

BENJAMIN: Yes, obviously.

DAVID: No, I *swear*. And then, like, halfway through, I was like: Wait a minute. This might actually *be* something. And so . . . I showed it to my agent.

BENJAMIN: And what did he say?

DAVID: He said, "This is about your friend Ben, isn't it."

BENJAMIN: Ha-ha.

DAVID: No, really, he did.

BENJAMIN: Oh.

DAVID: And, you know, seeing as this is more or less my livelihood, and how rare it is that one of these things comes out, you know, I figured . . .

BENJAMIN: Okay. *(Pause.)* And you never spit *water* all over me, that's ridiculous.

DAVID: Yeah, the actors added that. Spit take. I cannot convince them to take it out. Anyway, it kind of works. *(Pause.)* What exactly about that last scene made you walk out?

BENJAMIN: Why?

DAVID: I'm just . . . curious.

BENJAMIN: You know? I just kind of felt like I could see where it was going and I didn't like it.

DAVID: *Oh. (Pause.)* So, what, you felt like you were ahead of it?

BENJAMIN: Oh, please, I'm not—

DAVID: No, I know—

BENJAMIN: *(Overlapping)* I'm not giving you *notes* here, okay?

DAVID: *(Overlapping)* No, I know, I just—

BENJAMIN: *(Overlapping)* I mean, don't interpret this as the response of a casual audience member.

DAVID: Well, so, but was there a particular *line* that was the last straw, or . . .

(Beat.)

BENJAMIN: He told me to get the fuck out.

DAVID: He wasn't . . . talking to you personally.

BENJAMIN: I kind of felt like he was.

DAVID: I don't think that's fair.

BENJAMIN: Uh. Me either.

DAVID: *(Pause.)* I'll take another look at it.

BENJAMIN: So did you, uh . . . ?

DAVID: What.

BENJAMIN: Did you really *do* that?

DAVID: Yeah. Can you believe it?

BENJAMIN: Are you *crazy?*

DAVID: What's especially weird is that the director thinks that part is hilarious. Go figure: I do it in real life and I destroy my relationship with several colleagues. I put it into a play and it's everybody's favorite speech.

BENJAMIN: That whole . . . second Q and A with the, uh—

DAVID: Well, no, more just the speech *in* that scene. The interspersing of the phone calls, people are more uncertain if they like it.

BENJAMIN: Really? Because . . .

DAVID: What.

BENJAMIN: Well, I mean, *I* liked how the first time it happens, the two threads are contemporaneous, but the second time it happens it sort of bridges—

DAVID: You *got* that. I'm always so worried that that's going to *confuse* people.

BENJAMIN: Well, I mean, it *does*. It is. It's totally confusing. But I think that's okay, because it's sort of, uh—

DAVID: People kept telling me to *change* it.

BENJAMIN: Well, don't.

DAVID: Cool. *Thank you.*

BENJAMIN: It's just what I think. *(Beat.)* People?

DAVID: Yeah, random people who insist on terrible ideas. It's called "collaboration." Actually, the big one is people keep for some reason suggesting that one or both of them should be gay.

BENJAMIN: Well, theater people.

DAVID: Sure, literary fiction, very butch.

BENJAMIN: And they probably sense that one of them *is* gay.

DAVID: Right: you.

BENJAMIN: Right: you.

DAVID: No, right: you.

(They chuckle.)

BENJAMIN: Any reviews?

DAVID: Oh. Not yet. Later. I'm sure they'll be very mean.

BENJAMIN: I'm sure they'll be very nice.

DAVID: Right, so then they'll be mean the *next* time. Whatever, honestly, who *reads* that crap. *(Beat.)* Sorry about the ones for the movie, by the way.

BENJAMIN: I wasn't. I mean: I didn't write it. Right?

DAVID: Right.

BENJAMIN: Anyway, that's what they do. Is they build you up. And then they act like you did it to yourself and they knock you down.

DAVID: Yeah. *(Long pause.)* I'm sorry.

BENJAMIN: What? For what?

DAVID: I mean, just . . . Listen, is there anything you want me to . . . change, or take out, or—

BENJAMIN: What? No, don't be ridiculous, that's not . . . It's *your—*

DAVID: Sure, sure, but: seriously, goodwill gesture. Would it make you feel better if I maybe . . . changed something?

BENJAMIN: I . . . *(Beat.)* You don't have to. But since you asked. Some of that stuff, about, like . . . *(Pause.)* Um, I guess, kind of where he says that thing about "all these girls who want to be novelists." I mean, *all* of the borderline misogyny, sort of, but that especially, you could just, maybe, tone it down.

DAVID: *(Overlapping)* I'll see what I can do.

BENJAMIN: Just . . . My *wife* could see this, you know?

(Beat.)

DAVID: I'm sorry. Your what?

BENJAMIN: Oh. Um. *(He waggles a ringed finger.)* Yeah.

DAVID: *Wow. (Pause.)* Wow. Hey. Congratulations.

BENJAMIN: Thanks. Thank you.

DAVID: Uh . . . Who the hell is she?

BENJAMIN: This, uh, this girl I went to college with. Got back in touch with her a year or so ago. So. *(Pause.)* We should all get together for dinner.

DAVID: Oh . . . well, uh . . . *(Pause.)* Sure.

BENJAMIN: What?

DAVID: Nothing. *(Pause.)* You beat me at everything.

BENJAMIN: What?

DAVID: No. No, you just . . . You beat me *to* . . . everything. And then you tell me everything that's wrong with it before I get there.

BENJAMIN: What do you *mean?*

DAVID: I don't know.

BENJAMIN: Well, me either.

(Pause.)

DAVID: Hey. Why don't you go back inside?

BENJAMIN: Oh, no—

DAVID: Just for the last scene.

BENJAMIN: I'm missing it already.

DAVID: Actually, no, right now you're missing the *second*-to-last scene. Which is maybe just as well, it's one I'm *really* not sure of, the play gets all . . . *(Pause.)* Anyway, no, there's one more scene after that. So. Just . . . Look, let's start over. Just go in and watch the last scene.

BENJAMIN: Why?

DAVID: I just . . . I want you to see it.

BENJAMIN: Okay. *(Pause.)* I mean, I paid the ridiculous price for this shit.

DAVID: Next time, call me. I'll comp you in. *(Pause.)* Come on.

BENJAMIN: I don't want to disturb people, like . . . finding my seat.

DAVID: We'll go around the side. We'll watch from there.

(Pause.)

BENJAMIN: Okay.

(DAVID goes to the door and opens it. At this, perhaps there is a shaft of light from behind the audience, as though a door has also opened at the back of the theater. DAVID holds the door for BENJAMIN, who enters and then follows him in . . . the lights shift . . .)

SCENE NINE

(Ten years earlier. The crest of a hill in the woods at night.)

*(*DAVID *and* BENJAMIN, *in scruffy camp clothing, crest the hill. They stare out.)*

BENJAMIN: Well.

DAVID: Right?

BENJAMIN: This . . . rocks.

DAVID: Yeah, it does. It does.

BENJAMIN: Although it's also sort of . . . contrived?

DAVID: What do you mean?

BENJAMIN: Oh, you know, last night of camp, so let's have a big dramatic ritualistic event and get everybody worked up and teary-eyed.

DAVID: Sure. But it works.

BENJAMIN: It definitely works.

(BENJAMIN lights a cigarette behind DAVID's back.)

DAVID: Very discreet.

BENJAMIN: It's like World War One. You have to keep the ember hidden, pointed away from the enemy.

DAVID: What are the counselors gonna do *now*? Send you home?

BENJAMIN: Tell my parents.

DAVID: Right. *(Pause.)* Isn't it weird to think that in, like, ten years, we could very well be musicians?

BENJAMIN: What do you mean?

DAVID: Just that . . . you know . . . it's weird to think that.

BENJAMIN: We already *are* musicians.

DAVID: I just . . . You know . . . to be doing it for real.

BENJAMIN: This is real.

DAVID: You know what I mean.

BENJAMIN: I really don't.

DAVID: Well, I appreciate that about you.

(Pause.)

BENJAMIN: Hey: in eighty years we'll both be dead.

DAVID: I guess that's true. *(Pause.)* In *forty* if you keep smoking those.

BENJAMIN: Want one?

DAVID: No thanks.

BENJAMIN: Come on. Try one. Just one.

DAVID: I . . . No. No thank you.

BENJAMIN: You'll like it.

DAVID: What is this? An after-school special?

BENJAMIN: Um. No. Here.

(BENJAMIN *offers a cigarette.* DAVID *takes it.)*

DAVID: I don't . . . I don't even know how to . . .

BENJAMIN: What?

DAVID: Smoke.

BENJAMIN: I'll teach you.

(Pause.)

DAVID: All right.

BENJAMIN: Light it.

DAVID: How?

BENJAMIN: You have to be inhaling it as you light it.

DAVID: See, that's the part I don't know how to do.

BENJAMIN: *(Overlapping)* Right, right, take mine.

(BENJAMIN *hands* DAVID *his cigarette.)*

DAVID: What now?

BENJAMIN: Okay. Think of it as two separate maneuvers.

DAVID: Think of what?

BENJAMIN: Inhaling.

DAVID: Okay.

BENJAMIN: First you pull the smoke into your mouth. First part. *Then* you inhale it into your lungs. Second part.

DAVID: Okay.

(DAVID attempts this. He exhales. He tries again. He exhales.)

BENJAMIN: Eh?

DAVID: That's, uh . . .

BENJAMIN: Right?

DAVID: That's really, really . . .

BENJAMIN: I know. Then, once you're better at it, you get to the point where you can sort of naturally do both at once. Like breathing. *(Pause.)* Soon, I'll get you started on the harder stuff.

DAVID: I can't wait.

(Pause. They smoke.)

DAVID: You want to hear something weird that I do?

BENJAMIN: Probably not.

DAVID: Well, anyway: sometimes? I'll go into a record store? And, like, imagine a band name, like think of the name of whatever my band is going to someday be, and then go to the spot in the rock section, you know, alphabetically, where my albums would be, and imagine a whole bunch of them there, and how it would look in the store, and what bands it would be in between, and, you know, the titles for the albums, and the cover art . . .

BENJAMIN: Huh.

DAVID: Is that weird?

BENJAMIN: I don't know. *(Pause.)* You know what we should do?

DAVID: What's that?

BENJAMIN: We should form a band.

DAVID: What?

BENJAMIN: Well, that way, we'll have a project together, that we're working on, and it will provide, you know, an *excuse* to keep in touch.

DAVID: Do you think we need that?

BENJAMIN: Everybody needs that.

DAVID: Okay. *(Pause.)* But . . .

BENJAMIN: What?

DAVID: It doesn't make any sense.

BENJAMIN: Why not?

DAVID: Because we live across the country from each other.

BENJAMIN: So?

DAVID: So how are we going to rehearse?

BENJAMIN: I guess . . . independently.

DAVID: How are we going to write songs?

BENJAMIN: Maybe . . . play each other riffs over the phone.

DAVID: How are we going to record a demo?

BENJAMIN: I could lay down my tracks, mail the DAT to you, you do yours. Cobble it together—

DAVID: I don't think that's how bands work.

BENJAMIN: So?

DAVID: And, I mean: there's just the two of us.

BENJAMIN: Okay.

DAVID: And we both play keyboards.

BENJAMIN: Right, but—

DAVID: I just . . . I don't think it would work.

BENJAMIN: Hey. Okay.

(Pause. Suddenly, BENJAMIN *breaks down sobbing. He cries with surprising violence.)*

DAVID: Hey! . . . Hey . . . Hey, what's wrong?

BENJAMIN: I just . . .

DAVID: What?

BENJAMIN: Dave! You're going to be *across the country.* Do you *realize* what that *means*?

DAVID: I . . . don't know. What does it mean?

BENJAMIN: It means . . . It means . . . *(Beat.)* Why aren't *you* crying?

DAVID: I don't know! *(Pause.)* Benjamin.

BENJAMIN: What?

DAVID: We're friends. Okay? We're friends. We don't need an excuse.

(Pause.)

BENJAMIN: Okay.

DAVID: It's too bad we didn't meet a year ago. We could have gone to college together.

BENJAMIN: No, that's probably good, actually.

DAVID: Why?

BENJAMIN: Because, you know: each time we *do* get to hang out will be more . . .

DAVID: No, right. You might be right.

BENJAMIN: Of course I am.

(Pause.)

DAVID: Can I have another cigarette?

BENJAMIN: *(He chuckles.)* Okay.

DAVID: What's so funny?

BENJAMIN: You. You have this very funny . . . you're a little bit reluctant to try new things, and then once you do, it's like you invented it, and you exhibit no self-control at all. So now you're going to chain-smoke.

DAVID: Well, we'll see about that.

BENJAMIN: Yes we will.

(BENJAMIN stands and lights another cigarette for DAVID.)

DAVID: Hey, what about the enemy?

BENJAMIN: Let 'em come.

(Pause. DAVID gestures expansively to the valley below.)

DAVID: "Someday, Simba. All of this. Everything the light touches. Will be part of your kingdom."

BENJAMIN: What the hell are you talking about?

DAVID: Dude. Disney? *The Lion King*? You never saw it?

BENJAMIN: Um. No.

DAVID: Oh, you should, man. It's genius. Genius.

(DAVID and BENJAMIN stand side by side, looking down, beyond the crest of the hill, at the glow of the bonfire . . .)

(. . . and, as the lights fade, the last flickers of the flames illuminate another pair, in silhouette, dressed in suits, faces lost in shadow, watching from the wings . . .)

(Fade to black.)

Johnathan look
Cody chucklec
My friend Pam
me where the cast
As we got to
had two acts and
no intermission, w
of it. Also, a cou
needed to be swap
a Problem Scene,
son simply didn't
our day off betwee
On our day of
Johnathan attempt
of them, I forget v
the highway (low
from somewhere t
etc.) until we foun
where Cody and I
rejects every oppo
past to which you
gamble. *(Pause.)* A
Cody wins money
him to explain.
"It has a lot to
"but even more to
Shortly after t
Angeles.
Shortly after th

"So there's a play
"Yeah."

Notes

A NOTE ABOUT DOUBLING

I've seen a couple of different solutions for the doubles at the end of the play and I liked them both. In Pam MacKinnon's production at the Old Globe in San Diego, a second pair of actors were present in a "moat" around the stage for the whole play, helping with scene and costume changes, wearing the costumes that the actors were to wear in the final scene. The doubles exited the space entirely only at the end of Scene Seven, when David yells at everyone to get out, and then reentered at the top of Scene Nine in the actors' costumes from Scene Eight, in a doorway visible to the audience, in silhouette so that they were not immediately identifiable as the doubles. If that makes sense. This bought time for the actors to quick-change for the final scene, and then they surprised the audience when they entered for it while seemingly simultaneously being elsewhere in the space, which was a neat bit of theatrical sleight of hand. In the play's East Coast premiere, at 1812 Productions in Philadelphia, Pete Pryor and his designer, Jorge Cosineau, used video projections of shadows against the back wall of the stage, as though the actors were standing at the back of the house in an

lier, for a previou
The first was two
initial workshop o

That worksho
Pfaelzer had left
San Francisco. A.(
me into a playwri
who actually wor
might be someth
charge to the way
ater offices. On t
gional production
yet clear whether
sustaining career.
was spending a fa
again, my sister ha
when he was one

The Four of U
David and Benjan
friends of mine. I
they had both, at
a role I'd based v
cause Cody was l
this workshop wa
them friends with
indestructible trio

Around the ta
"It's always so ex
loud for the very

*Tony Kushner's *Ang
1995.

†For the record: Crai

"I feel like it's working, within what I've got, toward something."

"Sure."

"As opposed to, This is a disaster."

"And write a new play."

"And write a new play."

"I agree."

Tony and I, along with Berkeley Rep's literary manager, Madeleine Oldham, were at a bar called Jupiter,* engaging in the customary post-rehearsal retire-to-the-bar-to-talk-about-the-play portion of the day.† I nodded thoughtfully at their notes and wrote everything down while trying to appear agreeable and, simultaneously, stubborn and also unconcerned, and everybody at the table knew that I would have no idea what was useful, or even what was true, until weeks or months later. I also began to listen carefully for how frequently Tony was using the word "when," as in "when we produce this play," as opposed to "in," as in "in a real production," as though my tallying these instances might later carry actual contractual weight.

TONY: The play is too long, for one thing.

ME: Well, I mean, there would be trims and streamlining. Over the course of a, um, full rehearsal process.

TONY: Well, sure, but you don't want to be *in a real production situation* before you find out if you can even cut it down to size.

ME: *(Sotto voce)* Damn.

TONY: What was that?

*Because I moved away from Berkeley at eighteen, I only really know the cafés and will never be totally comfortable at the bars. The mental map of where to go to drink alcohol and feel old and talk about resignation to the facts of the present feels to me like an ill-fitting superimposition over the map of where to go to drink lattés and feel young and talk about thrilling plans for the future. So the bars there feel like dreams of my hometown to me. New spaces that are not quite right.

†There go my late nights. So much for Denise's introduction.

ME: I said: "You're right. Hopefully our focus on what is in the play's artistic interest will incidentally also address any 'produceorial' concerns."

TONY: It is in the artistic interest of the play that it be shorter.

ME: *(Sotto sotto voce)* You ever say that to Kushner?

TONY: What was that?

Later, after ranting about Society for a while,* Tony left.

Madeleine and I stayed. She asked me why I was staring into space, and for some reason I told her. I said that although I'd always struggled in my relationships with women with feeling somehow cut off from myself or from the world, I was beginning to suspect that ideally, a second pair of eyes on your life can actually expand its meaning, whereas trying to make do with only your own eyes is unfulfilling because your life is unshared, and trying to imagine a hypothetical audience of others out there in the universe is unfulfilling because you know you've made it up. Or that maybe, since no matter how complicatedly you put this kind of thing it's still pretty much a self-evident nugget of non-wisdom, this idea had shifted from being something I knew intellectually to something I acutely felt. On the heels of which had arrived the attended fear of, Okay, wanting it is one thing, but still, What If I Just Can't Do It?

Madeleine, who is married, pushed her cat-eye glasses up her nose and said, "You know what the hard thing about realizing something like that is? It doesn't make it happen any faster. And also? You won't know if you can do it till you're in it."

I said, "By the way? Tony was my ride. You're going to have to drive me home."

---

*"That you guys come out of school tens of thousands of dollars in debt is a crime! People should be executed! It's two generations of indentured servitude now!"

It's 1:00 a.m. on a Wednesday, and Berkeley is beyond dead, and the street outside the bar is an abandoned movie set that looks exactly like where I grew up.

My road trip with Cameron was actually our second. The previous summer, we'd gone from west to east across the North, and the plan this time was to close the circle, as it were, and go from east to west across the South. On the first trip, our travel through a vast external space (the redwoods near the Oregon border; a lake in Idaho called Pend Oreille; endless Montana) was mirrored for me, to my surprise, by an equally searching internal exploration. I couldn't avoid thinking and feeling very deeply about my life, in other words, and I freaked out. But it was a mini-crisis that ultimately left me clearer and somehow healed when I came out the other side. I'm self-conscious about how this might sound, goofy or pretentious, but it's the truth. So naturally, on our second trip I went in expecting a similarly epiphanic experience. I even had a short mental list of the epiphanies I expected to have, and I spent the first few days being very frustrated with myself for failing to have them. And when thoughts and feelings did begin to bubble up from some hidden deep, they weren't the ones I'd planned on. That's not, it turns out, how epiphanies operate. Or: Sometimes you do The Work and sometimes The Work does you.

The Four of Us premiered at the Old Globe Theatre in San Diego in February of 2007. Things had changed some for me by then. My play *Bach at Leipzig* had appeared Off-Broadway, and the self-sustaining career I'd been after seemed to be more or less under way, which mainly just served to create the space in which to worry about all kinds of new things, like Why Am I Doing This? and Is This All There Is? and What If All Of This Has Been In Every Sense A Terrible Mistake?

The Four of Us had changed some too, but the Problem Scene had persisted in remaining a Problem Scene for, literally, years. I had cut it, added to it, instructed actors to do it faster, put jokes into the play explicitly about the Problems with the Problem Scene, removed those jokes (wisely), and was nearing the point where I start saying things like, Hey, eventually you just have to move on and get it right on the next play.

I didn't even really have time to fix the Problem Scene anyway. I had a play called *Yellowjackets* that was much too long, and I was trying to cut it down in anticipation of a workshop scheduled for September. I was also working on what felt like it might be the beginning of something, called *Completeness*, about the love life of a computer scientist,* which was naturally just an excuse to write semi-obliquely about myself, and so I was unearthing some pretty volatile emotions while also having a hard time ridding myself of the shame associated with thinking and feeling very deeply about people who may have totally forgotten about you and then making those thoughts and feelings public. Also, while I was on the West Coast I was supposed to spend some time in L.A. having the kinds of meetings about television work in which people say "We want to be in business with you" and then never call you ever again.

The Problem with not fixing the Problem Scene, though, was that our actors, Sean and Gideon, were having to heft the thing onto their backs every day in rehearsal and carry it around, attempting to cloak its humiliating shortcomings with their own innate talent and charisma, while I watched, acutely aware that the Problem Scene was soon going to be exposed to paying audiences, who would then demand to know who was responsible.

Suddenly, it became clear how to fix it.

The Problem Scene had, basically, three sections, and they were,

---

*"Sounds like a short play!" Ha-ha-ha. You are not the first person to think of this joke.

I realized, arranged exactly backward. It made no sense for David and Benjamin to talk about music and then about girls and then about writing, because this was a progression that began with the wordless and moved through the emotional to arrive at the intellectual. And, because writing is meaningful only insofar as it expresses other, deeper concerns, which is to say that The Work is necessarily subordinate to, or just a conduit for, or a way of driving at, things that really matter, I was buttoning the scene with the thing that mattered least. Moreover, because actually engaging with deeper concerns in fact takes effort, I needed to earn the middle of the scene with whatever was at the beginning of the scene. I moved the beginning to the end, and the end to the beginning, and left the middle where it was so that the scene could go from lots of words about words to a topic for which language is insufficient to pure sound. Then I recused myself from the rehearsal room so that I wouldn't start rewriting the rest of the scenes out from under everybody just because I needed something to do.

Sean and Gideon were offended.

"So you're leaving rehearsal because you hate us and we're terrible." This is what actors hear no matter what you say.

"No. I think the thing's in really good shape and I think I'll be more valuable as a fresh eye during tech and previews."

"So we're terrible."

Pam buried her face in her hands.

Just before previews, Joanna Pfaelzer appeared. Her husband, Russell, was our lighting designer, and she'd come down from the Bay Area to see what had become of the play she'd helped shape. Her son, now two and a half, was with her. During a break in tech, the actors having moved from positions they'd held for an hour to collapse into the seats, the little boy tottered down through the house and his father helped him step across the gap onto the stage. The jet-black deck reflected the boy, whole and upside down. Joanna told us that soon they were all going to move back to New York. Her time at A.C.T. had run its course. The break ended. Sean and Gideon rose from the audience, got back onstage, and froze again so that Russell could set all his cues, lighting this moment perfectly before moving on to the next.

Toward the end of my week in Berkeley, just before the public readings began, I walked around Berkeley High School. I mean literally "around," because the place is by now so well fortified that I couldn't figure out how to get onto the campus. So—although the hope, I guess, was that soaking up some of the current ambience of the place would gird me in authenticity, the better to prepare for the post-show talk-backs full of current Berkeley residents, once I was there it became clear how lame a notion that really was. Then the phone in my pocket rang. It was Johnathan. This actually happened, I swear.

"Hey, brother."

"Hey. I've been writing about you a little bit."

"Oh no. Why's that?"

"I'm doing the introduction to *The Four of Us*, and I'm telling revealing anecdotes."

"I don't want to know. How's the workshop of *Yellowjackets* going?"

"We'll see. He's still saying 'in' more often than he's saying 'when.' How's L.A.?"

"Oh, fuck this place," he said. "I am so out of here."

"Right."

"Seriously. That's the other reason I'm calling. I'm going to finish up this show I'm doing right now and then I'm moving back to New York. In like a few months."

"Awesome. Why?"

Johnathan said that working in L.A. was moving him further and further away from the reasons that he'd started acting in the first place and toward a version of himself that he wasn't sure he wanted to be.

"So I just, uh. I just can't live in Los Angeles," he said. "Anymore."

On our second road trip, Cameron got really annoyed at the frequency with which I crack my knuckles. Apparently I do this about once every twenty minutes.

(Crack.)

"Okay. You're going to have to stop doing that."

"I don't do it that often."

"Once every twenty minutes. Every twenty minutes for nine days."

(Crack) "Sorry!"

"Oh my God. You have to stop. Have to stop that. Also, it's terrible for you and it's hard to watch you do that to yourself over and over and over again."

For the last day or two of the trip, I would catch my hands hovering near each other and it took superhuman effort to keep them apart. And then my attention would wander.

(Crack.)

"It's just an insult now. It's not even about the knuckle-cracking anymore. Now it's just like every time you do that, you're saying, 'Cameron? Fuck you.' "

On the last day, I didn't crack my knuckles once. It was torture.

"Aren't you proud of me?"

Cameron shrugged as if to say, Congratulations, you made a sensible decision for once in your life.

"I like the play. I want to do it."

It was my last night in Berkeley, just after the final public reading of *Yellowjackets*, and Tony had pulled me aside.

"Oh, I didn't realize we were trying to decide that. I was just focusing on the artistic—"

"Shut up. So, next season. Fall of 2008, maybe—I don't know exactly, we'll have to figure that out—but let's do it."

We shook hands and smiled in a complicated kind of relief: at the fact that he hadn't had to let me down and at the fact that I had done my work and it had been enough and at the fact that this week wasn't the end of something but now seemed just a preamble to something even better. I walked outside. It was early evening on a Sunday, and Berkeley was not empty now. The buildings popped the way buildings do in evening light. Off to one side, near the entrance to the theater, all our young actors were still standing around together, frozen in the last moment of the experience, not wanting to say goodbye, too young to know that in this business—in this life, even—there really only ever seems to be goodbye-for-now.

That night, back at my parents' house, my sister called and put her son, now three, on the phone. He was talking now, really interacting, like a real little person, like his own self.

"Goodbye, Uncle Ee-tomorrow," he said.

In the background, my sister prompted him: "Travel safe."

"Trava-say!"

I packed my suitcase in the living room, surrounded by younger versions of myself. Then I called Denise and told her she could have her introduction, as long as we could put it at the end, where it belonged.

The Four of Us is a play about a friendship between two writers over the course of about ten years. It unfolds out of chronological order because sometimes that's the best way to land the inscrutable connections between things. People ask me if the play is autobiographical, if there's a Benjamin in my life; or, more often, more recently, if there's a David; or, sometimes, if the play is really just a conversation with myself. The answer is yes. I wrote the first draft in a café in Brooklyn three and a half years ago, about fifteen blocks from another café, where I am sitting and writing the end of this introduction right now. And you are not reading this until, at the earliest, March of 2008, when the play is scheduled to open in New York.* I wish I could tell you what happens then. But I don't know yet.

What a writer makes public is at best a truthful but partial and fragmented glimpse of a private conversation that is happening all the time. Sometimes out loud, with friends or lovers. Somewhat more often in silences, with those people or alone. So listen, you. It's clear now that a silence is about to open up between us. I can see the blank bottom of the page from here. And I don't know how long it's going to last because it's not entirely up to me. And you're already reaching for another book and I'm about to start something new. So here's the part I need for you to understand. I want to tell you everything. I want to tell you absolutely everything about absolutely everything and that is why I do this and it never works. All I ever seem to do is tell you over and over and over again about the wanting. All I ever do is introduce the things I really want to say. Which are unsayable with words. Which are not pure bursts of feeling and of sound, but which want to be, for you.

Travel safe.

Bye for now.

(Crack.)

ITAMAR MOSES
Berkeley, CA–Brooklyn, NY
September–October 2007

*Unless, of course, you are Denise.